People in Britain
A CENSUS ATLAS

PREPARED BY

Census Research Unit
Department of Geography
University of Durham

IN COLLABORATION WITH

Office of Population Censuses
and Surveys, *and*
General Register Office (Scotland)

HER MAJESTY'S STATIONERY OFFICE

Authors

**Census Research Unit, Department of Geography,
University of Durham**
John I. Clarke
John C. Dewdney
Ian S. Evans
David W. Rhind
Mahes Visvalingam

assisted by
Jane Coulter
Barbara Perry
Kate Stanness

Office of Population Censuses and Surveys
Chris Denham

Acknowledgements
The completion of this atlas would not have been possible with-
out a substantial research grant from the Social Science Research
Council, to whom thanks are gratefully accorded.

Numerous people have helped at various stages in the making of
the atlas and in carrying out the associated statistical processing.
In particular we wish to thank the following:

University of Durham, Department of Geography
Mrs J. Dresser, Messrs A. Corner, D. Hudspeth, J. Normile,
I. Middlemass, D. Ewbank and D. Cowton

Office of Population Censuses and Surveys
Miss A. Brown, Dr C. Hakim, Mrs S. Wileman, Messrs G. Boston
and A. Clark

University of Durham Computer Unit
Messrs B. Lander and R. Sheehan

Seiscom Delta Ltd
Mr P. Ferrar

f301.32942

-7. MAY 1981

11690618 9 \ 8102

DR

Contents

Foreword   *page* 1

Introduction
Grid referencing in the 1971 Census of Population   3
Assigning grid references   4
Statistics for grid squares   4
Number of squares mapped   5
Computer mapping   5
    Absolute number maps   6
    Maps related to the national average (signed chi-squared)   6
    Special cases   7
    Producing the maps   7

Part 1   National maps of Great Britain
List of maps   9
Introduction   10
Demographic maps   10
Socio-economic characteristics   10
Household characteristics   11
Comparisons and contrasts   11
Regional variations   11
Base map   13
Maps and commentary   14

Part 2   Regional maps
List of maps   85
Introduction   87
Maps and commentary   90

Appendices
1 Definitions of the variables selected for mapping   122
2 The use of the signed chi-squared measure for mapping   124
3 National and regional averages for the variables mapped   126
4 The distribution of squares among mapping classes   127
5 Publications of the Census Research Unit   132

Foreword

The maps of *People in Britain* give a unique view of the spatial distribution of our population and of its characteristics. They are the result of applying new techniques to new data. They bring out national, regional and local patterns from the wealth of detail provided in the 1971 Census of Population. We feel that publication of this Atlas, ranging as it does over most of the questions asked in the Census, will play an important part in making the Census available to a wider public, and in particular to schools and colleges.

The maps complement the statistical reports we have made to Parliament. They do not themselves present precise figures; these are in our statistical tables. Rather the maps demonstrate at a glance, in a way tables cannot, the spatial patterns and the variations and similarities across the surface of Britain. They prompt questions about interrelationships — not just between the various characteristics plotted, but also with such geographical features as relief, geology, climate, economic development, communications, urban structure and so on. Although the census data from which the maps have been compiled were collected nine years ago, the patterns revealed by the maps change only relatively slowly. They are still likely to apply in large measure today.

The maps are drawn from statistics for the one kilometre squares of the National Grid. These squares are unchanging through time, a virtue that is not shared by administrative areas. A second virtue of grid squares is their spatial regularity. Grid squares were used in a population census for the first time in 1971, and we hope to produce statistics for the squares again in the 1981 Census. Grid squares offer the prospect of a decennial series of statistics for an unchanging geographical base, so yielding patterns both in space and time.

Making the maps would have been impossible without computers to marshal the statistics and to guide the map plotting devices.

But, as is often the case, what appears in the Atlas as a fairly simple presentation of key statistics is in fact the result of a substantial design effort; the research work, which was supported by a grant from the Social Science Research Council, is reflected in the list of published working papers. Users of this Atlas will be able to judge the effectiveness of the techniques adopted — for example, the chi-squared analysis featured in many of the maps. Users' comments to the team that produced this Atlas will be welcome.

People in Britain is the result of collaboration between members of the Institute of British Geographers at the Census Research Unit in the University of Durham and staff of our two Offices. The individuals who have been principally involved are mentioned in the opening pages. The Census Research Unit has carried out the major task of making the maps from the statistics supplied by the Census Offices, and has prepared the commentary accompanying the maps. We are particularly grateful for the Unit's contribution to this Atlas.

A R Thatcher
Registrar General for England and Wales

V C Stewart
Registrar General for Scotland

Introduction

The maps in *People in Britain* give a unique view of the spatial distribution of our population and of their characteristics. They synthesise national, regional and local patterns from the wealth of detail provided in the Census of Population and range over most of the questions asked in the 1971 Census.

They are the result of applying new techniques to new data. The maps are based on statistics for one kilometre squares of the National Grid, available for the first time in a population census. Making the maps would not have been possible without computers to marshal the statistics beforehand and to guide the laser plotter used to make the symbols for the squares.

This introduction describes the National Grid system of location referencing and how census statistics were compiled for grid squares. It discusses the statistics available for grid squares — statistics which are essentially the same as those available for other small areas. It goes on to explain the types of map in the atlas and the techniques employed for producing them.

The maps of *People in Britain* are in two groups. First, 34 maps of Great Britain cover population distribution and density, birthplaces, other demographic characteristics, socio-economic characteristics, travel to work and households and housing. Second, larger scale maps in groups of four cover each of seven of Britain's most populous regions. Four appendices give details of the statistical bases of the maps.

Grid referencing in the 1971 Census of Population
The introduction of a system of grid squares for location referencing in the 1971 Census of Population in Great Britain was associated with one of the most significant trends in the analysis of census material: the study of populations in small geographical areas. The Census was the third in succession (1961, 1966, 1971) from which a standard set of statistics for small areas was produced — the Small Area Statistics. At the same time there has been a demand for more flexibility in the geographical base for census statistics, combined with a demand for continuity which is not given by administrative areas or by the enumeration districts used in taking a census. The grid squares have the very considerable advantage of remaining unchanged through time.

After extensive trials and consultation with census users during 1968 and 1969, it was decided that the National Grid should be used as an alternative geographical base. Thus the 1971 Census became the first in which a National Grid co-ordinate reference was added to every address enumerated in Great Britain. The purpose was to obtain statistics for populations in National Grid squares of 100 metres or one kilometre, the positions of which are generally available from Ordnance Survey maps. Such squares can be used as a common spatial base for various sets of data.

The National Grid system extends over a rectangle 1300 km by 700 km entirely covering Great Britain and is based on a special projection so that the grid lines are distinct from, but can be related to, lines of longitude and latitude. The regularity of the grid facilitates the statistical anlysis of spatial patterns and the display of patterns through automated cartography.

Assigning grid references
In the Census, buildings were assigned by the enumerators to a particular National Grid square using up-to-date large scale Ordnance Survey maps. In England and Wales, buildings were assigned to 100 metre squares in areas mapped at scales of 1:1250 or 1:2500 (these maps show individual buildings and their addresses) and to one kilometre squares in areas mapped at scales of 1:10,000 (buildings in clusters are not always clearly distinguished at this scale). In Scotland, it was possible to assign buildings to 100 metre squares in all areas because of the generally dispersed nature of settlement in areas mapped at 1:10,000. Enumerators were able to find the vast majority of buildings on their maps and referencing was of a high standard. In cases of uncertainty, where the enumerator could not assign a building to a grid square, the reference was added to the records at census headquarters. The whole process was subject to systematic checks for accuracy.

Thus the great majority (98.7 per cent) of census schedules arriving at headquarters carried the grid square reference of the building in which the particular household was enumerated. Grid square references were put on magnetic tape with the main census data. At that stage in processing, individual records were grouped within households and household records within enumeration districts. The population of a grid square was often scattered over a number of enumeration districts, and the major operation of sorting the data into grid square order and their aggregation into grid square statistics had to take place as a secondary exercise after the main tables for conventional area sets had been completed. Because of this and other delays in the system, the grid square statistics only became available some five years after the 1971 Census.

Statistics for grid squares
The maps in *People in Britain* are based on the standard Small Area Statistics (SAS) for each one kilometre national grid square, which may be purchased from the Census Offices. These Small Area Statistics are virtually identical to those produced, and widely used, at the enumeration district, ward and parish level. The value of SAS for enumeration districts as nationally comparable statistics for small areas had, however, been limited in part by the difficulties of identifying the location of each small area beyond the single National Grid reference given for the centre of the area. The statistics for grid squares remove this problem.

The characteristics of the Small Area Statistics have developed in response to a variety of demands from users, though some characteristics reflect the way the statistics have to be produced. Steps must also be taken to ensure that information about identifiable individuals is not disclosed. Nevertheless, the standard SAS for one kilometre grid squares, while imposing some limitations on the topics which could be mapped in the atlas, provided an excellent data base for the atlas.

The SAS refer to populations smaller than those reported in the published volumes of the census, but the topics range over the whole content of the census. The tables are much abbreviated versions of tables available for larger populations in published census reports: broad classifications are used and the number of dimensions in the tables is limited. The 1971 Census SAS consisted of approximately 1500 counts arranged into cross tabulations with a maximum of 72 cells and four dimensions, together with 48 ratios.

There were two sets of data for each area: data which were easy to code such as age, sex and economic status and of which 100 per cent were processed; and the data which required more time-consuming and skilled coding – a person's workplace, industry, educational qualifications and so on – of which a 10 per cent sample were processed. For the latter, one household was selected at random from each run of ten households within an enumeration district, and one person in ten was similarly chosen from those not in households. The 1971 Census SAS were therefore divided into two sections, one with tables drawn only from 100 per cent data and a section with tables including 10 per cent data. The 100 per cent section was further divided into tables covering the characteristics of people (the population tables) and tables covering the characteristics of households (the household tables).

The 10 per cent samples of households and of individuals not in households were *not* reselected from the populations of grid squares; this was to avoid the cost and delay of further coding. Samples in squares with reasonably sized populations and containing the whole or parts of a number of enumeration districts will usually be near 10 per cent. But in squares with small populations, perhaps containing only parts of enumeration districts, the sample may be much higher or much lower than 10 per cent or it may be zero.

Returns from the 1971 Census were processed sequentially, area by area. SAS for enumeration districts, wards and parishes were produced and issued in this sequence, before the returns from the country as a whole had been processed. It was not possible to include figures at that stage about people normally resident in an area but away on census night and enumerated elsewhere because their schedules might have been among those for part of the country not yet processed. Similarly it was not possible to include figures about people living elsewhere but working in an area, or about people who had moved from an area to another part of the country. It was, moreover, impractical later on to re-allocate the data for absent residents back to grid squares or to code addresses of workplace and previous residence to grid squares. Thus the standard SAS for grid squares relate to people and households present on census night, as indeed do the SAS for enumeration districts. There are counts of absent households and the total of rooms in them, but data about absent residents are not included. Data about visitors are also excluded from most figures. All statistics about people's occupations, journeys to work, and so on, relate to the area where people live rather than to the areas where they work.

Number of squares mapped

On Census night in April 1971 people were enumerated in 147,685 one kilometre squares. Map 1 shows these squares. Basic counts of the numbers of households, males and females are available for these squares. Maps 3 and 9 and one map for each region included in this atlas are based on these counts. However, to preserve confidentiality and avoid the disclosure of information about identifiable persons or households, 100 per cent population tables are not released for squares with fewer than 25 people, nor household tables for squares with less than eight households. As a further safeguard applied to all 100 per cent tables, a quasi-random pattern of +1, −1, or 0 has been added to figures in the individual cells. Where there is only one household in the 10 per cent sample for a square, the 10 per cent tables are not released. Where tables are not released for a square, the term *suppressed square* is used; where tables are released, the term *unsuppressed square* is used.

The pattern of settlement in Britain gives a highly concentrated or skewed distribution of population over grid squares – in 1971, one quarter of Britain's population was crowded into 30 out of the total of 2700 populated 10 kilometre squares and a further one hundred 10 kilometre squares accounted for another quarter. With one kilometre squares the distribution is still more uneven. The resultant frequency of suppression and the variability of population size within the grid squares required the development of special techniques for presenting grid square statistics.

The maps of demographic characteristics are based on 67,546 unsuppressed one kilometre squares; those of household characteristics are based on 68,422 unsuppressed one kilometre squares; and those of occupation, socio-economic groups and travel to work are based on 10 per cent sample tables for about 54,300 unsuppressed one kilometre squares. The number of one kilometre symbols on a particular map may be less; for example, the variable shown in Map 12, *Persons over retirement age,* is males aged 65 and over plus females aged 60 and over in private households per 10,000 persons in private households, and there were 65,021 unsuppressed one kilometre squares in which there were private households. The variable shown in Map 10, *Fertility of young married women,* is the number of children ever born to married women aged 16–29 in private households per 1000 such women; there were 58,479 unsuppressed one kilometre squares with such women present.

Computer mapping

The immense task of mapping such information necessitated the use of computers. Yet the detail of these maps is so great that, had each one-kilometre square been represented by a single 2.5 × 4.2 mm print character using the line-printer for computer output, as in certain mapping methods, each map of Britain would have been at least 4 metres high.

To produce the maps in this atlas, each grid square was allocated to a category on the basis of the variable being mapped. Each category was plotted on photographic film by laser beam at high resolution and final size, and then printed in a different colour. This made it possible to produce national maps from very detailed data, though only solid colours rather than tones of any one colour, had to be used to distinguish between squares with different characteristics. With one-kilometre squares, local variations can be picked out and the generalisation which results from the use of information for large units, such as local authority areas, can be avoided.

Our aim in making the maps has been to highlight the contrasts between different parts of Britain. Thus, even where the number of individuals involved is relatively small, as in Map 8 *New Commonwealth parentage* and Map 18 *Miners,* the categories or classes to which the squares are allocated were chosen to show areas of concentration. The resulting maps may be just as densely coloured as any map of the total population. The actual numbers of people and squares involved are given in the texts accompanying the maps and in the appendices, as necessary background to assessment of the variations mapped.

A number of important decisions had to be made in the course of preparing these maps, such as which particular variables should be mapped and what method should be used to portray them. The sections below describe how and why these decisions were made.

i) Absolute number maps

Eight of the national maps in this atlas (Maps 3, 5, 6, 7, 8, 17, 18 and 34) are based upon actual numbers in each one kilometre square – for example Map 3 showing population density and Map 18 showing numbers of miners. Each square is allocated to one of four or five classes with a given range of numbers. For each variable, there are many squares with small numbers and a few squares with large numbers. To prevent most squares falling into a single class, giving maps showing little differentiation, the classes used increase in width for increasing numbers. Thus the birthplace maps (restricted to squares which in total have 25 or more people) show squares with no people of the particular birthplace (yellow); squares with 1–10 people of the particular birthplace (blue); squares with 11–50 (red) and squares with more than 50 (black). The last class contains very few squares, but covers a broad range of numbers of people: for example, only 9.59 per cent of the 67,420 mapped squares have more than 50 Welsh-born, but the square with the maximum number has 8550. For comparability, the same class limits have been used for all birthplace maps (Maps 5–8) and, for example, only 3.67 per cent of mapped squares have more than 50 people of New Commonwealth parentage. On Map 3 *Population density* all inhabited squares are coloured, and uncoloured squares have no inhabitants (see also Maps 1 and 4). On other absolute number maps, uncoloured squares include not only those with no inhabitants, but also those for which detailed data are suppressed.

ii) Maps related to the national average (signed chi-squared maps)

Some populations (people with certain birthplaces, or occupations for example) are concentrated in relatively few areas. These populations have been mapped as absolute numbers and differences from the distribution of total population can be seen. Other populations are more widely distributed and consequently a map of absolute numbers of – say – old people would closely resemble a map of total population. Conventionally such populations have been mapped in relation to a 'control' population: old people in relation to the total population; semi-skilled workers in relation to 'economically active'; owner-occupied households in relation to total private households; and so on. In such maps, the variable mapped has usually been defined as a ratio such as 'old people divided by total population', which varies from zero to one (or zero to 100 per cent).

The ratio method was considered, but rejected as being far from satisfactory for mapping grid-square data. Squares with small populations tend to have high or low ratios more frequently than squares with larger populations, while squares with large numbers of people tend to have ratios closer to the national average. Thus ratio maps for populations in grid squares often show very little variation among the densely-populated grid squares where most people live and in which the reader may have considerable interest. Moreover, because the statistics for the larger populations are less subject to errors, it is preferable to emphasise their characteristics rather than extremely variable ratios in sparsely peopled areas.

Also rejected was the mapping method which would have shown how many more or fewer people with a particular characteristic there were in each square than the number expected from the national proportion of people with that characteristic. In such maps, squares with few people are unlikely ever to fall into extreme classes, because it is impossible for the number to be great. Just as ratio maps can have a bias towards showing contrasts in thinly peopled areas, the deviation maps are biased towards showing contrasts within urban areas.

The problem of mapping unevenly distributed populations with widely varying characteristics has been solved in a novel way, which we believe to have broader applications: by combining absolute and relative deviations from the number expected, to give a chi-squared map (as explained further in Appendix 2). Since we have retained the sign (+ or −) of the deviation above or below average, these maps are described as *signed chi-squared maps.* Our signed chi-squared maps have four classes so that the national proportion of people with the given characteristic can be used as the mid-point of the scale. These maps can thus be read as two-class ratio (or deviation) maps, distinguishing those one kilometre squares with values above the national average (purple and blue) from those with below average values (red and yellow).

The further subdivisions into *above average* (blue) and *high* (purple) and *below average* (yellow) and *low* (red) are based upon the chi-squared criterion. The chi-squared method takes account of deviations from expectation in *both* ratio *and* absolute terms and forms a compromise between these two extremes. A square with a large population will be placed in the high (purple) class if the proportion with the chosen characteristic is only moderately above average, the numbers with the chosen characteristic in excess of expectation being, however, substantial. By contrast, a square with a small population will be placed in the high (purple) class if the proportion with the characteristic is substantially above average, the numbers with the characteristic in excess of expectation being relatively moderate. This is shown diagrammatically in Figure 1. The signed chi-squared criterion, then, is based upon both the ratio and the number involved, producing a useful compromise between a ratio map and a deviation map. The method has been used for 22 of the Great Britain maps and for three of each set of four regional maps.

Fig 1   The signed chi-squared criterion

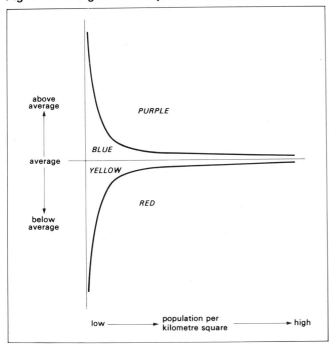

The same colour scheme is used for all the signed chi-squared maps, making the maps easier to compare. It is interesting, however, that the colour impression given by the maps varies: between a stark purple/red contrast, as in Map 27 *Council tenants,* and more modestly shaded blue and yellow pictures in Map 21 *Unemployed men* and Map 16 *Unskilled manual workers*. These contrasts reflect variations in the number of squares in each mapping class. Where large numbers of people or households are involved and grid squares are polarised between those with many

and those with few (as for council-tenant households and other tenure variables), most squares fall into one or other of the extreme classes — red and purple. There are more near-average squares which are shown in blue or yellow where numbers are small, as for all variables from the 10 per cent sample data, and for relatively small groups such as *Unemployed men,* Map 21, or in Map 31 *Overcrowding,* or where there is less polarisation, as Map 33 *One-person households*. These important variations would have been lost if class intervals based upon equal percentiles had been used.

iii) Special cases
A number of our maps do not fall into either of the two main types discussed so far: unique mapping systems have been used in these special cases and are explained in the accompanying texts. Maps 1 and 2 are single-class maps showing all populated squares and all unsuppressed squares respectively; Map 4a *Population per 10 km square* is a block diagram of population distribution; Map 9 *Sex composition* shows only the two extreme (very high and very low) classes; Map 13 *Types of age structure* is unique in giving an overall picture of the age composition of the population rather than mapping a single age-group.

iv) Producing the maps
The intricate detail provided by one kilometre squares has been exploited by the use of a novel technique which employs a laser beam to draw the maps directly at the scale of reproduction.[1] This technique has been used in several recent atlases,[2] but the high resolution produced for this atlas by laser plotting is unequalled to date. Indeed, such high-resolution maps simply could not have been produced without the laser-plotting technique.

Given the very large numbers of squares which make up the maps in this atlas the speed of automated devices linked to a computer is obviously required. Certain devices, for example character printers, produce maps of relatively low visual quality. With photo-reduction the quality of such maps can be improved,[3] but these maps deal with far fewer data points and simpler patterns than those portrayed in this atlas. Other devices, such as the pen plotter,[4] would have been too slow for maps of the whole of Great Britain.

The technique used in the production of *People in Britain* involved repeated scanning of a sheet of film by a laser beam. The beam passed to and fro across the film, covering all the areas occupied by grid squares along one west-to-east row. To scan the next row of squares, the film was moved up by an appropriate amount — a quarter of a millimetre for the Great Britain maps. The beam was only switched on for squares falling into a particular class (to be represented by a single printing colour). This produced a sheet of transparent film which was black only where a particular colour was to be printed. Three such films were plotted and used to make printing plates for the three printing colours, blue, yellow and red. Purple was obtained (for the signed chi-square maps) by overprinting blue on red, green by blue on yellow, brick red by red on yellow, and black by a combination of all three primary colours.

In the national maps in this atlas, Great Britain is plotted at a scale of approximately 1:4 million (precisely 1:3,936,000). The Shetland Islands are placed in an inset east of Aberdeen, while the Orkneys and Thurso area are shown both on the main map and, to provide continuity with the Shetlands, in the inset. At this scale, each one kilometre square is one hundredth of an inch across (0.254 mm), and is plotted by four tiny adjacent dots arranged in a square. Choice of colour is restrained by cost and also because each grid square is so small that printing plates cannot be screened to give a paler shade; each must be printed as a solid colour.

The plotter starts in the north-west corner and plots eastwards, then moves south to the next row of data, and so on to the south-east corner. This 'raster plotting' is especially suitable for data in grid square format. The plotting on film is at the printing scale to avoid the need to enlarge or reduce photographically. The plotter, owned by Seiscom Delta Ltd, was driven under instructions from a magnetic tape written on the IBM 370/168 computer owned by the Universities of Durham and Newcastle (NUMAC: Northern Universities Multiple Access Computer). Before this tape could be written, the Census Research Unit at the University of Durham had to undertake a great deal of computer processing of the data supplied by the Office of Population Censuses and Surveys, which comprised the full SAS file for each one-kilometre square. This very large data set required initial translation and compaction for storage and use on the NUMAC system.[5] New variables were constructed as possible items for statistical analysis and mapping, and the final selection of variables to be mapped in this atlas was carried out with the aid of preliminary plots on a cathode ray storage tube.

Such detail inevitably meant that the technology at the time of production was being strained to near its maximum capability. Very small perturbations in the laser scanning have given rise to small variations in scale within the map, producing the small gaps between some adjacent squares, such as in the map of 'Bath deficiency' on page 105. But 'technology' also includes the reproduction of many copies by conventional printing methods from the laser-produced film. The three-colour images must be aligned to within one fifth of a millimetre throughout a map to print correctly; copying the laser images even by normal high quality photograhic processes can give rise to infilling, where individual 'white' squares are surrounded by 'black' ones – hence some spurious colours can be created although others are due to optical illusions. By far the most common of these overlaps is between blue and yellow areas, producing green; on the signed chi-square maps any green will be where adjacent areas are just above and just below the national average value and hence will not detract from the important patterns on the map.

With computer-generated maps of the type used in this atlas, the author makes a general specification for a map, but does not know how this will translate exactly into mapped patterns until the map emerges from the laser plotter. The colour patterns and the variations in dominant colour from map to map arise from differences in the frequency distributions of the individual variables and in their spatial patterns. The speed and economy of automated mapping makes it possible for the author to specify a relatively large number of maps, then select a smaller set of the most telling. Thus the author intervenes in a different way from that encountered in conventional cartography.

References
1   Rhind, D. W. High speed maps by laser beam, *Geographical Magazine* May 1974, 393–4; Rhind, D. W., Visvalingam, M., Perry, B. J. and Evans, I.S., People mapped by laser beam, *Geographical Magazine* Dec. 1976, 148–52.

2   Coates, B.E. *Census Atlas of South Yorkshire,* Department of Geography, University of Sheffield, 1974; Dewdney J.C. and Rhind D.W. (eds.) *People in Durham – a census atlas,* Census Research Unit, Department of Geography, University of Durham, 1976.

3   Rosing, K. and Wood, P.A. *Character of a Conurbation: A Computer Atlas of Birmingham and the Black Country,* London University Press, 1971.

4   Used for some of the maps in Dewdney and Rhind, *op cit.* 1976.

5   Visvalingam, M. Storage of the 1971 U.K. Census data; some technical considerations, *Working Paper No. 4,* Census Research Unit, Department of Geography, University of Durham, 1975; Visvalingam, M. and Perry, B.J., Storage of the grid-square based 1971 G.B. Census data; checking procedures, *Working Paper No. 7,* Census Research Unit, Department of Geography, University of Durham, 1976; Visvalingam, M., A locational index for the 1971 kilometre-square population census data for Great Britain, *Working Paper No. 12,* Census Research Unit, Department of Geography, University of Durham, 1977.

PART 1
National maps of Great Britain

Introduction   *page* 10

Population
1   Populated squares   14
2   Unsuppressed squares   16
3   Population density   18
4   Population per 10 km square   20
4A Population per 10 km square: a bird's eye view   22

Birthplaces
5   Born in Scotland   24
6   Born in Wales   26
7   Born in the Irish Republic   28
8   New Commonwealth parentage   30

Demographic characteristics
9   Sex composition   32
10 Fertility of young married women   34
11 Children   36
12 Persons over retirement age   38
13 Types of age structure   40

Socio-economic characteristics
14 Educational qualifications   42
15 Foremen and skilled manual workers   44
16 Unskilled manual workers   46
17 Farmers, foresters and fishermen   48
18 Miners   50
19 Manufacturing workers   52
20 Managerial and professional workers   54
21 Unemployed men   56

Travel to work
22 Car to work   58
23 Bus to work   60
24 Train to work   62
25 Walking to work   64

Households and housing
26 Owner-occupiers   66
27 Council tenants   68
28 Private tenants   70
29 Household amenities   72
30 Households with no car   74
31 Overcrowding   76
32 Spacious accommodation   78
33 One-person households   80
34 One-parent families   82

Introduction

The variables mapped for the whole of Great Britain were selected after 102 variables had been mapped in monochrome as ratios. These 102 variables were established by aggregation and selection from the 1571 counts available from the SAS for each unsuppressed one kilometre square[1]. The 102 variables covered most of the information contained in SAS, by aggregating, for example, age data into broader groups. The further reduction to 34 variables to be mapped in this atlas was achieved by comparison of the 102 ratio maps and study of correlations between the variables. Except for the groups of variables judged to be most important (for example, types of household tenure, modes of travel to work), only one representative variable was selected from each cluster of interrelated variables.

The patterns on Maps 1, 2 and 3 are basic to the understanding of all subsequent maps. Map 1 shows all populated squares, while Map 2 *Unsuppressed squares* shows all one-kilometre squares for which the full range of population data were available. The broad pattern on Map 3 *Population density* is reflected in all subsequent maps. For example, many maps show concentric variations around city centres, which can be located on the population density map, and contrasts between urban and rural areas. However, as 100 per cent SAS of population other than the numbers of persons, males and females are available only for squares with 25 or more people, the pattern on Map 2 *Unsuppressed squares* provides a more precise areal base for subsequent maps derived from the 100 per cent population SAS. Maps based on the 10 per cent SAS display a slightly different pattern from those of the 100 per cent population SAS owing to the different suppression procedures used, but bear a strong resemblance to the pattern on Map 2.

Demographic maps

These maps show people's birthplaces, variations in the sex and age composition of the population, and variations in the fertility of young married women.

The 1971 Census included questions on the country of birth of each person and the countries of birth of his or her parents. There are three maps of persons' birthplaces. Two of the birthplace maps, *Born in Scotland* (Map 5) and *Born in Wales* (Map 6), show great contrasts between the country of origin and the rest of Great Britain. Map 7, *Born in the Irish Republic* does not show such a contrast, since the population is of external origin. Map 8, *New Commonwealth parentage,* is based upon the data of birthplace and parents' birthplaces.

While birthplaces were mapped by absolute numbers, the signed

chi-square method seemed more appropriate for other demographic variables. Among the latter, *sex composition* (Map 9), which rarely varies greatly from the national ratio of males to females, is the only one available for all 147,685 populated squares. From the rather limited fertility data provided in the SAS, we have chosen to map the *fertility of young married women* (Map 10), which is more varied and distinctive than the fertility of older groups of women. Of a large set of possible groupings of the population by age, two groups are mapped, namely *children* (Map 11) and *people over retirement age* (Map 12). These groups are of considerable importance in the provision of social services and have more distinctive distributions than other age-groups; a map of the very old (75 years and over) proved to differ very little from that of the population over retirement age, and was not included in the atlas. In an attempt to sum up the very complex nature of age structure variations among the British population, a multivariate map *Types of age structure* (Map 13) has also been included.

Socio-economic characteristics

Variables of social and economic significance are available in abundance. To show the distribution of educationally qualified people, those with degrees and equivalent qualifications were combined with those holding GCE or related qualifications in Map 14 *Educational qualifications*. *Foremen and skilled manual workers* (Map 15), *Unskilled manual workers* (Map 16) and *Managerial and professional workers* (Map 20) cover broad socio-economic groupings; they demonstrate the main variations in the spatial distributions of such groups, and it was found that maps of semi-skilled manual workers and other non-manual workers added little to the picture.

Employment in three contrasting industry groups was mapped. *Farmers, foresters and fishermen* (Map 17) and *Miners* (Map 18) provide distinctive distributions on the basis of absolute numbers, while *Manufacturing workers* (Map 19) is a signed chi-squared map, since the distribution correlates more closely with that of total population. To complement the picture of those at work at the time of the Census, *Unemployed men* (Map 21) were mapped.

Dominant modes of travel to work relate to regional life-styles and are a primary concern of planning. Four maps are included, covering the main modes: *Car to work* (Map 22), *Bus to work* (Map 23), *Train to work* (Map 24) and *Walking to work* (Map 25). The minority groups of workers travelling to work by motor cycle (1.5 per cent) or pedal cycle (4.2 per cent) were not mapped.

Maps 14–20 and 22–25 are based on 10 per cent sample figures. The sample was drawn as 10 per cent of the households in each enumeration district so that, although the method of stratified sampling normally ensured that sample households were scattered throughout an enumeration district, the percentage of households sampled in each grid square may be significantly above or below 10 per cent. Despite these imperfections, the resulting maps show perfectly reasonable and interpretable distributions.

Household characteristics

Among the 100 per cent household variables, types of tenure underlie many other distributions. Our maps of tenure show three classes: *Owner-occupiers* (Map 26), *Council tenants* (Map 27) and *Private tenants* (Map 28), the last being a combination of the two census categories 'furnished, privately rented' and 'unfurnished, privately rented'.

The joint presence of the three basic amenities (hot water, fixed bath and inside wc) is shown in *Household amenities* (Map 29). Map 30 *Households with no car,* shows the absence of a means of transport which has important implications for personal mobility. Two maps cover the extremes of crowding in terms of persons per room, namely *Overcrowding* (Map 31) and *Spacious accommodation* (Map 32). Of many possible variables related to household size and composition, *One-person households* (Map 33) and *One-parent families* (Map 34) were felt to be of particular interest; other household size variables are predictable from the age structure, especially the number of children[2].

Comparisons and contrasts

Certain features are common to many of the national maps in this atlas. The first is undoubtedly the detailed and intricate influence of relief and altitude upon the overall pattern of population distribution, whether we look at Map 1 *Populated squares,* Map 2 *Unsuppressed squares,* Map 3 *Population density* per one kilometre square or Map 4 *Population per 10 km square.* Moreover, the general division between highland Britain and lowland Britain is strongly revealed. Within highland Britain, the only major population concentrations are in Central Scotland, North-east England and South Wales, and there are very large uninhabited areas. In contrast, the spread of population distribution in lowland Britain is much thicker, especially in the axial belt from London in the south east, through the Midlands to Lancashire and West Yorkshire, which incorporates five of the seven major 1971 conurbations.

Certain categories of population and households are particularly concentrated in the conurbations, including those with certain birthplaces (Maps 5–8), *Households with no car* (Map 30),

Overcrowding (Map 31), *One-person households* (Map 33) and *One-parent families* (Map 34); indeed the concentration is so marked in the case of one-parent families that the map picks out the cores of conurbations and other urban areas and is like an urban population map of Great Britain.

Many maps show core-periphery contrasts within the major conurbations: for example, *Children* (Map 11), *Persons over retirement age* (Map 12), *Types of age structure* (Map 13), *Unemployed men* (Map 21), *Car to work* (Map 22), *Walking to work* (Map 25), *Owner-occupiers* (Map 26), *Private tenants* (Map 28), *Household amenities* (Map 29), *Households with no car* (Map 30), *Overcrowding* (Map 31), and *One-person households* (Map 33).

Four fifths of the population of Great Britain live in towns and the urban populations stand out on these maps by containing extreme values in the various classifications – black or brick-red on the absolute number maps, purple or red on the chi-squared maps. In contrast, the rural populations, with lower densities, are mostly characterised by yellow or blue squares, though a military establishment or a large institution can transform the population composition. For highly polarised distributions, like those in Map 24 *Train to work* and Map 27 *Council tenants,* patterns in rural areas are visually simple, but for maps of more evenly distributed variables, such as *Fertility of young married women* (Map 10), *Children* (Map 11), *Persons over retirement age* (Map 12) and *Car to work* (Map 22), rural areas have very complex patterns of colours.

Regional variations

Certain parts of Great Britain and types of regions also stand out on many of the maps. London and the south east is characterised by populations with rather older than average age structure (Maps 10–13), concentrations of those with *educational qualifications* (Map 14), *managerial and professional workers* (Map 20) and people who take a *train to work* (Map 24). Scotland, on the other hand, is characterised by younger than average age structures (Maps 10–13) and concentrations of public authority housing (Map 27) and crowded households (Map 31). Similarly, coalfields are visible on many maps, not merely on Map 18 *Miners* and Map 19 *Manufacturing workers,* but also on *Foremen and skilled manual workers* (Map 15), *Bus to work* (Map 23) and *Council tenants* (Map 27) as well as, in a negative sense, on *Educational qualifications* (Map 14) and *Managerial and professional workers* (Map 20). Another strongly marked regional type is the coastal retirement area, seen in *Sex composition* (Map 9), *Age structure* (Maps 10–13), *Owner-occupiers* (Map 26) and *Spacious accommodation* (Map 32), as well as negatively in several others such as *Manufacturing workers* (Map 19) and *Overcrowding* (Map 31).

Further regional variations may be seen in the regional maps in the second part of this atlas — pages 85–120.

Base map

Because each data area (one kilometre square) is so small, it was not feasible to print a detailed base showing, for example, roads or town names on the Great Britain maps: such an overprint would have obliterated much information. The sea is distinguished from unpopulated or suppressed squares, which are white. The pattern of white squares is itself a base map of sorts, though it does differ as between those maps showing all 147,685 populated squares (Maps 1, 3 and 9); other maps derived from 100 per cent population data, where there are 67,546 unsuppressed squares; maps derived from the 100 per cent hosehold data, with 68,422 unsuppressed squares; maps based on the 10 per cent sample, where the number of unsuppressed squares is 53,277. Such differences do not affect the visual impression of general distributions, but it is helpful to make cross-reference to Map 1 *Populated squares,* Map 2 *Unsuppressed squares* and Map 3 *Population density.* As a further aid to the reader, a key map indicating the position of major towns is also included.

References

[1] Rhind, D.W., Evans, I.S. and Dewdney, J.C. The derivation of new variables from population census data, *Working Paper No. 9,* Census Research Unit, Department of Geography, University of Durham, 1977.

[2] Evans, I.S., Relationships between G.B. census variables at the 1km aggregate level. Forthcoming in *Statistical Applications in the Spatial Sciences,* N.J. Wrigley (ed), Pion, London.

MAP 1
Populated squares

This map shows, in a single colour, all the one kilometre squares which in 1971 contained population, however few people. It thus depicts, with great accuracy and detail, the pattern of population distribution in Great Britain at that date. To be precise, the map shows where people were present on Census night. Visitors were included with residents, but absent residents were excluded. Thus there were few squares with inhabited dwellings where everyone was away on Census night. The 147,685 inhabited squares on the map cover about two thirds of the land area of Great Britain. While the average population density for the country as a whole was 235 per sq km, for the inhabited squares alone it was 353 per sq km. Since density variations among the populated squares are not indicated in this map (but are shown and discussed in detail in Map 3 and the accompanying text), interest centres on the dichotomy between uninhabited (white) and inhabited (red) squares.

In the broad sense, at least, the pattern is clearly related to the physical environment and especially to altitude and relief. The largest white areas indicate the location of the main hill masses of highland Britain – the Scottish Highlands, the upland district of central Scotland, the Southern Uplands, the Lake District, the Pennines, the Welsh massif and, in the south west, the smaller massifs of Exmoor, Dartmoor and Bodmin Moor – are all clearly visible. In all these areas, the detailed pattern of local relief can be seen; every inhabited upland valley is faithfully portrayed by a string of populated squares. In the Scottish Highlands and Islands, strings of populated squares along the coasts are another striking feature. Smaller patches of empty upland territory can be distinguished within the English scarplands, notably in the Cleveland Hills and North York Moors, in the higher parts of the Cotswolds and along the South Downs. The large extent of empty territory on Salisbury plain is clear, the effects of relief being emphasised by the exclusion of population from military training areas. Lowland blocks of unpopulated squares include the Brecklands of East Anglia, the New Forest and such local features as Dungeness and the marshlands along the Essex and north Kent coasts.

Throughout most of lowland Britain, however, populated squares outnumber empty ones, and two contrasting patterns can be seen. These reflect, in part, the geological and physical grain of the landscape and, in part, the character of the settlement pattern. In some areas, the local distribution of population is such as to give numerous individual one kilometre squares with no inhabitants and thus an extremely complex pattern of red and white patches. This is particularly true of the scarpland zone extending from east Yorkshire and Lincolnshire through the East Midlands into Wiltshire and Dorset, where the population tends to

be clustered in villages and where uninhabited squares are more numerous on the chalk and limestone uplands than in the intervening clay vales. A more solid pattern of red occurs in areas where the rural population is more evenly spread, regardless of actual density, as for example in East Anglia, the rural parts of the West Midlands, Pembroke and north east Scotland.

Solid blocks of colour cover the main urban areas, though even here occasional white squares do occur, as in west London, for example, where Heathrow airport can be identified.

Populated squares

0   km   100

MAP 2
Unsuppressed squares

The available data for squares with fewer than 25 inhabitants are restricted to counts of males, females and total population; all other population characteristics are suppressed (see page 5). This map shows the 67,543 squares with 25 or more inhabitants for which the *full range* of 100 per cent SAS population data are available. The unsuppressed squares constitute only 46 per cent of the 147,685 populated squares shown in Map 1 and, at first sight, there may appear to be a major deficiency in our data base and thus in our maps. However, these unsuppressed squares contain no less than 98.5 per cent of the total population of Great Britain – at an average density of about 780 people per sq km. In short, although more than half the one-kilometre squares known to be inhabited do not appear on most of our maps, the 'missing' squares contain only about 1.5 per cent of the British population – some 800,000 people, widely scattered throughout the inhabited areas. Incidentally, the suppressed squares include virtually all those in the map of population density (Map 3) in the lowest category (yellow) – corresponding to populations of one to 25.

As might be expected, all the main urban areas stand out as continuous blocks of blue, though with the occasional white square marking the position of a major open space. Outside the conurbations, clusters of blue squares mark the more isolated urban centres and indeed many much smaller settlements in rural areas as well. Where rural densities are relatively high, the blue squares coalesce to give a more intricate pattern.

A great deal of local detail can be seen on this map. At the conurbation and major city level, the omission of squares with fewer than 25 inhabitants often gives a clearer picture of the urban structure. Thus in the West Midlands, for example, there is a clear break between Birmingham and Coventry which does not appear on the map of all populated squares, and in Yorkshire there is a break between Leeds/Bradford and Sheffield. In north east England, Teesside is clearly separated from other urban areas and even the narrow gap between Tyneside and Sunderland is visible. At the other end of the scale, small individual settlements can often be identified, as for example along the Fife coast from St. Andrews to Kirkcaldy, and in north east Scotland. In several cases there is a very clear picture of the local settlement pattern. A particularly good example is to be seen near the Wiltshire/Hampshire border in southern England. Salisbury stands out as a small block of blue squares, whence strings of blue squares run north west, north and north east along the valleys of the Wylye, Avon and Bourne. Slightly further north, the line of settlements at the northern edge of Salisbury Plain, overlooking the Vale of Pewsey can also be distinguished.

Though there are slight differences between the various maps in this atlas, since the number and distribution of unsuppressed squares varies, the pattern of unsuppressed squares for 100 per cent population data is very similar to that of unsuppressed squares for 100 per cent household data, because the distribution of population and households is closely related. The pattern of unsuppressed squares for 10 per cent data is also similar.

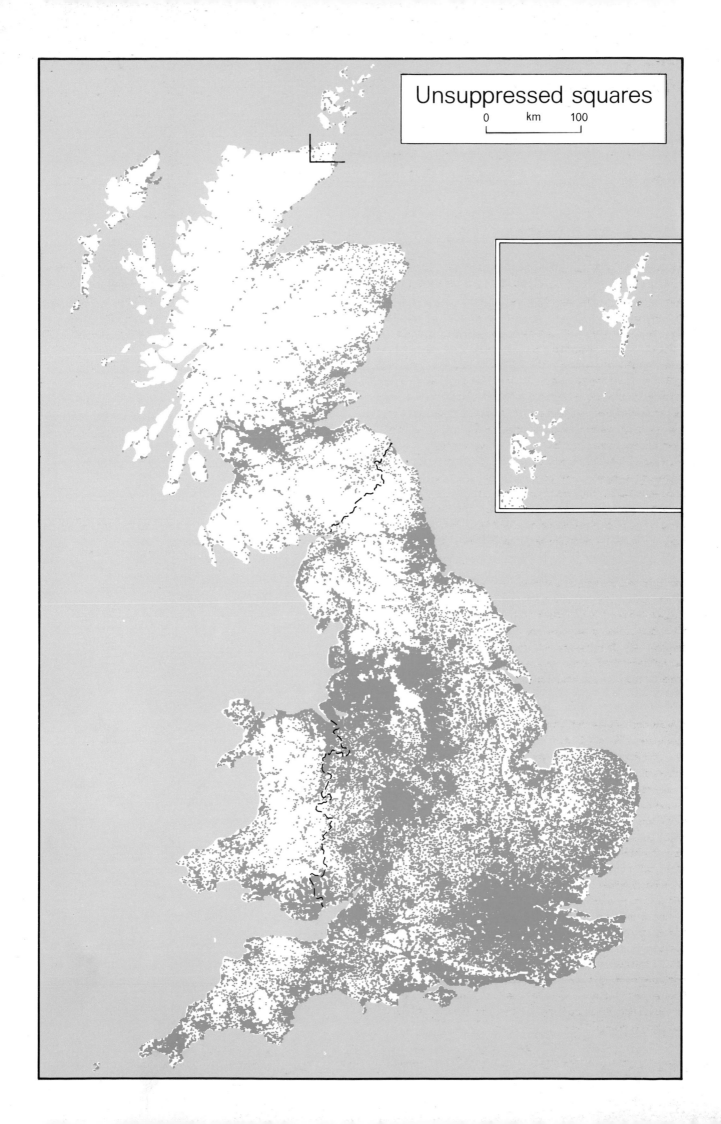

Unsuppressed squares

0   km   100

MAP 3
Population density

(Absolute numbers: number of people per kilometre square)

Maps of population density generally depict the average numbers of people per unit area for irregular administrative divisions rather than for regular grid squares. One great advantage of kilometre-square data is that, by plotting numbers for each kilometre square, a population density map is produced automatically. A major task in producing such a map for Great Britain as a whole, with such a wide range of population numbers in one kilometre squares, is to decide upon the number of density categories to be shown and the thresholds between them. Although the blanks on the map, depicting uninhabited squares, obviously remain the same whatever categories are chosen, the overall pattern of densities is greatly influenced by decisions on categories. In this particular map, the thresholds selected were at 25, 150, 800 and 4000 persons per square kilometre, a choice which was affected by the frequency distribution of values as well as by the relationships between population distribution and settlement patterns. The average populated one kilometre grid square has 365 people and thus falls within the middle of the five categories. While the great majority of the other maps in the atlas show only unsuppressed squares, this map depicts all the 147,685 populated one kilometre squares.

The lowest density category of 1–25 persons per square kilometre (yellow) includes those 84,897 squares for which only the total populations and the numbers of males and females are available. This lowest density category is characteristic of areas of dispersed rural settlement, the most extensive of which occur in the lowlands and valleys of Scotland, northern England, Wales and the south west. In the uplands, every inhabited valley is faithfully picked out by a string of populated squares. Almost all coastal squares are populated, marking out the coastline nearly everywhere except in parts of western Scotland. The lowest density category is also widely present in the English scarplands, northwards and eastwards from Dorset to the Yorkshire Wolds, where rural settlement is concentrated into nucleated villages and habitations outside the villages are often few and scattered. The Black Fens are also distinctly marked by a sweep of yellow squares.

The next two density categories of 26–150 (blue) and 151–800 (green) persons per square kilometre characterise rural areas with sizeable villages and the urban fringes. The sprinkled and linear patterns of rural settlements in the English scarplands and the more densely inhabited valleys of the uplands contrast with the solid areas of colour in districts with more uniformly distributed rural settlement such as eastern East Anglia. The two categories combine to give substantial areas of settlement in districts of

intensive agricultural activity, such as the silt Fens, and non-urban areas with mixtures of agriculture and other activities, such as the lowlands of Lancashire and Cheshire, the Severn vale, the Bristol-Somerset area, western Cornwall and the Weald.

Areas of well above average density, 801–4000 persons per square kilometre (red) and above 4000 (black), mark urban settlement. The cores of conurbations and larger towns are black; red shows the spread of suburbs and satellite towns, and pin-points virtually all settlements with more than 1000 inhabitants; red predominates in some areas of continuous but looser urban settlement such as the valleys of South Wales, parts of West and South Yorkshire and some seaside resorts. The most densely populated one-kilometre grid square is in the Earls Court area of London and has a population of 24,300, which gives a density of 243 persons per hectare.

A larger version of this density map on a scale of 1:1.3 million is published as a wallchart *People in Britain,* HMSO £1.95, available from Census Information Unit, OPCS, St. Catherines House, 10 Kingsway, London Wc2B 6JP.

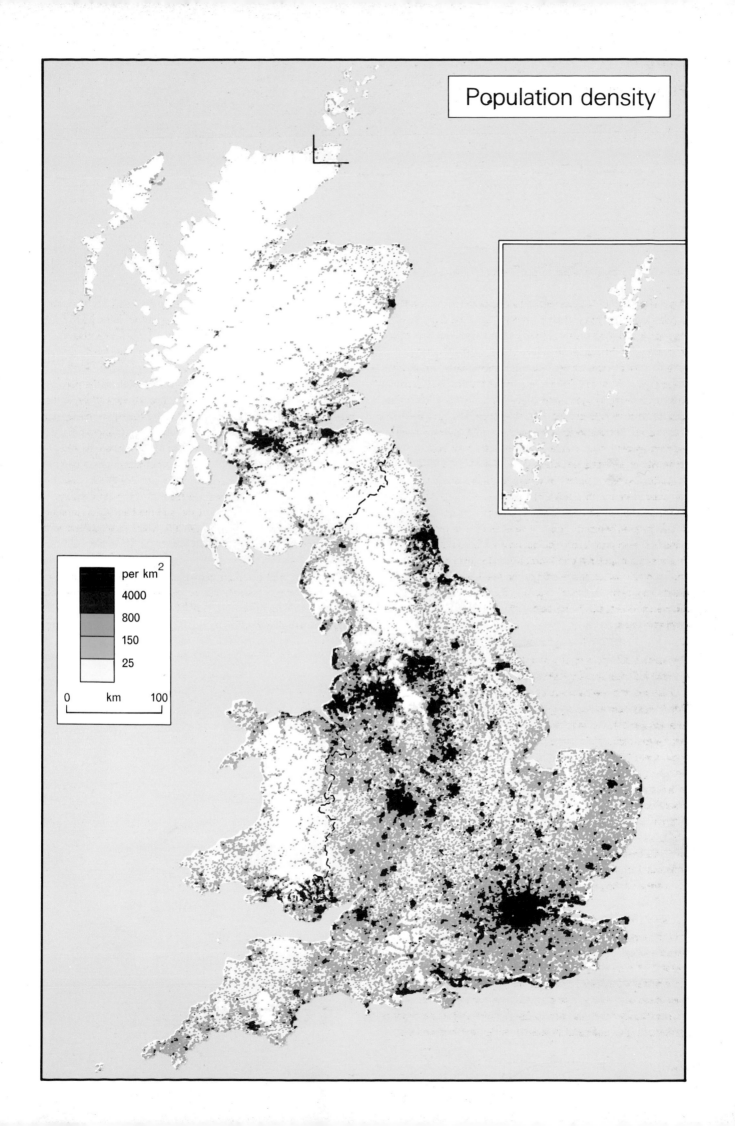

Population density

per km²
4000
800
150
25

0   km   100

MAP 4
Population per 10 km Square

(Absolute numbers: number of people per 10 kilometre square)

This map differs from all the others in this atlas in that, in place of the fine mesh of one kilometre squares, it is based on a much coarser grid of squares 100 times greater in area, each square measuring 10 km by 10 km. However, the class intervals used here are the same as on the one kilometre square population density map (Map 3), with break points at 25, 150, 800 and 4000 persons per square kilometre (that is 2500, 15,000, 80,000 and 400,000 per ten kilometre square). Obviously most of the fine detail shown in Map 3 is lost, but the map gives a very vivid picture of the general distribution of the population of Great Britain. The map does illustrate, however, the sometimes misleading effects of averaging populations over larger areal units.

Each square is coloured according to the average density over an area of 100 sq km and this masks a great deal of variation within the square. Moreover the population of the part of a coastal square that is land is averaged over the whole 100 sq km area; for example, a square that is 90 per cent sea and contains 2000 people has an average density of 20 per square kilometre and will thus be coloured yellow; in reality, the land area of that square has a density of 200 per square kilometre which places it in the next but one density class (green). Consequently, densities in coastal areas tend to be understated to a degree partly determined by the relationship of grid lines to the coastline.

Because of averaging, the white, unpopulated areas cover a much smaller part of this map than of Map 3 and are wholly confined to the Scottish Highlands. Fifteen unpopulated ten kilometre squares mark the highest areas of the Cairngorms and Central Highlands and there is a similar number of more scattered empty squares in the section north west of the Great Glen. Other mountain and upland areas fall mainly within the lowest density category of 1–25 persons per square kilometre or 1–2500 per ten kilometre square (coloured yellow), including most of the Highlands, the Southern Uplands, the Lake District, the northern Pennines, the Peak District and the Welsh massif. Smaller blocks of yellow squares occur on chalk and limestone uplands in England – the North York Moors, the Yorkshire and Lincolnshire Wolds, and Salisbury Plain, for example – and on the moorlands of Devon and Cornwall, and there are isolated yellow squares in the Brecklands and on the Sussex Downs.

The second density category of 2501–15,000 persons per ten kilometre square (blue) picks out the main rural/agricultural areas. In Scotland, blue squares occur around the north eastern edge of the Highlands, in the central lowland and in the Tweed basin, and rural areas of north and south Wales are also mainly in this category. In predominantly highland areas, single blue squares mark the position of the main settlements: in north and west Scotland, for example, it is possible to identify the squares containing Kirkwall, Thurso, Wick, Stornoway, Fort William, Oban and Campbeltown. In England, blue squares or those of higher densities cover virtually all but the most northerly areas.

Squares with 15,001–80,000 inhabitants (green) cover most of the main urban-industrial areas, as in Central Scotland, North East England, South Lancashire/West Yorkshire, the Midlands, South Wales and London. They also denote lesser population clusters of varying kinds such as the west Cumbrian coalfield, Barrow-in-Furness, Bristol, Torbay, and many others. The greatest concentration of green squares occurs in the axial belt from Lancashire and Yorkshire, through the Midlands to London and beyond.

Set within the green areas are blocks of squares with 80,001–400,000 inhabitants (red), denoting the more densely populated parts of the main urban agglomerations, Clydeside, Tyneside, South Lancashire, Leeds/Bradford, Sheffield, Nottingham/Derby, Birmingham and the Black Country, and London are all clearly visible. Blocks of two or three red squares denote such diverse centres as Dundee, Edinburgh, Teesside, Blackpool, Swansea, Cardiff, Bristol, Southampton, Bournemouth and Brighton, while single red squares identify, for example, Aberdeen, Norwich, Ipswich, Cambridge, Oxford, Swindon, Exeter and Plymouth.

Finally, only 13 ten kilometre squares (black) have more than 400,000 people each. Clydeside, Tyneside, Merseyside, Manchester and Birmingham each have one and the remaining eight are in central London. These 13 squares, covering approximately 0.6 per cent of the land area of Great Britain, contain approximately one tenth of the British population.

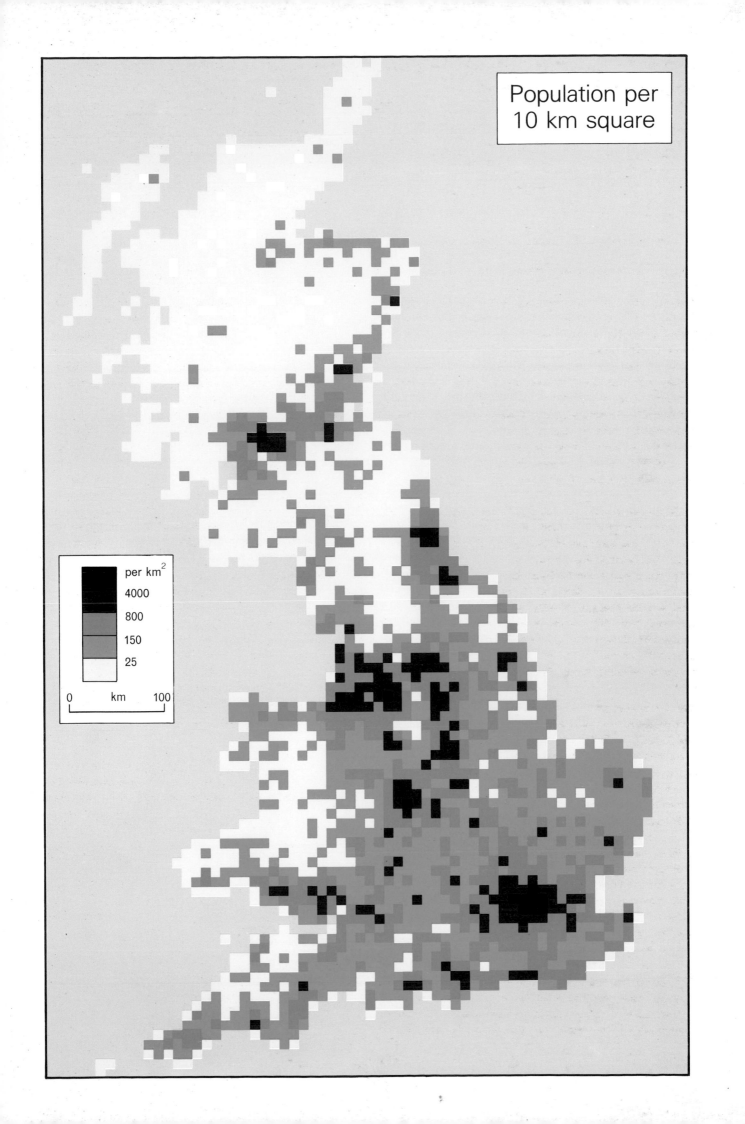

Population per
10 km square

per km²
4000
800
150
25

0   km   100

Population per 10 km Square:
A bird's eye view

(Absolute numbers: number of people per 10 kilometre square)

This diagram represents the same data as Map 4, but viewed as a block diagram in three dimensions rather than as a conventional map. There is a column for each national grid 10 km square, (an area of 100 sq km) and the height of the column is proportional to the number of people in that area. Britain is seen from over the North Sea (the view is oriented along a line 20° east of north), but there is no perspective in the diagram (the projection used is orthographic) and so the same numbers of people are shown as the same height of column everywhere on the diagram. The diagram was generated by the computer and drawn automatically, which included the erasure of all hidden lines.

The main centres of population are easily recognisable. Central London dominates the south, with nearly 900,000 people represented by the highest column. The Plymouth area is the major peak on the south western coast. Major peaks in the centre of the diagram are Birmingham, Manchester, Liverpool, Sheffield and Leeds-Bradford. Tyneside stands as an almost isolated island of high values on the north eastern coast (centre of diagram), while the relative sizes of the populations of Glasgow and Edinburgh are clearly seen. Aberdeen is the other high value square along the eastern coast and is the one nearest to the viewing point.

This diagram illustrates how, with computer graphics, the myriad facts available from the census can be organised in a very general, but very telling statement about the strongly marked pattern of population distribution and concentration in Britain.

Population per 10 km square – a bird's eye view

N

MAP 5
Born in Scotland

(Absolute numbers: People born in Scotland per kilometre square)

The 5,386,900 people born in Scotland represented 10.3 per cent of the resident population of Great Britain in 1971. Of these, 4,652,400 lived in Scotland, constituting 91.7 per cent of the population of that country, 716,500 lived in England (1.6 per cent) and 17,900 in Wales (0.7 per cent).

This map, like the other maps based on birthplace data, shows absolute numbers rather than proportions and the general pattern is therefore influenced by that of total population distribution.

The map of Scots, like that of Welsh (Map 6) shows the expected predominance in the country of origin, but also more significant patterns of distribution in the rest of Great Britain, which indicate selective migration. The larger, more prosperous centres of population are major points of attraction, particularly London. Other towns where there have been employment opportunities can be picked out. There have also been movements to certain retirement areas, though within reasonable reach of the country of origin. Penetration of rural areas declines with distance from the home country.

The map shows only those one kilometre squares with 25 or more inhabitants. A remarkably small number of such squares in Scotland had ten or fewer Scottish born: there are only about 20 blue squares (with 1–10 such people), scattered throughout the Highlands and Islands. Scots are found in rural areas of northern England, around London and in the East Midlands, but are poorly represented in rural Wales, East Anglia and the south west. The major concentration of Scots outside Scotland is clearly in London and its satellite towns and there are clusters in other conurbations. Medium and small urban centres with a sizeable Scottish element include Carlisle, Coventry, Leicester, Teesside, Scunthorpe and Corby. Scots also appear to be numerous in ports and centres of the armed forces (Plymouth, Southampton, Portsmouth, Aldershot) and in retirement centres, particularly those of northern England (Blackpool, Southport, Morecambe, Scarborough).

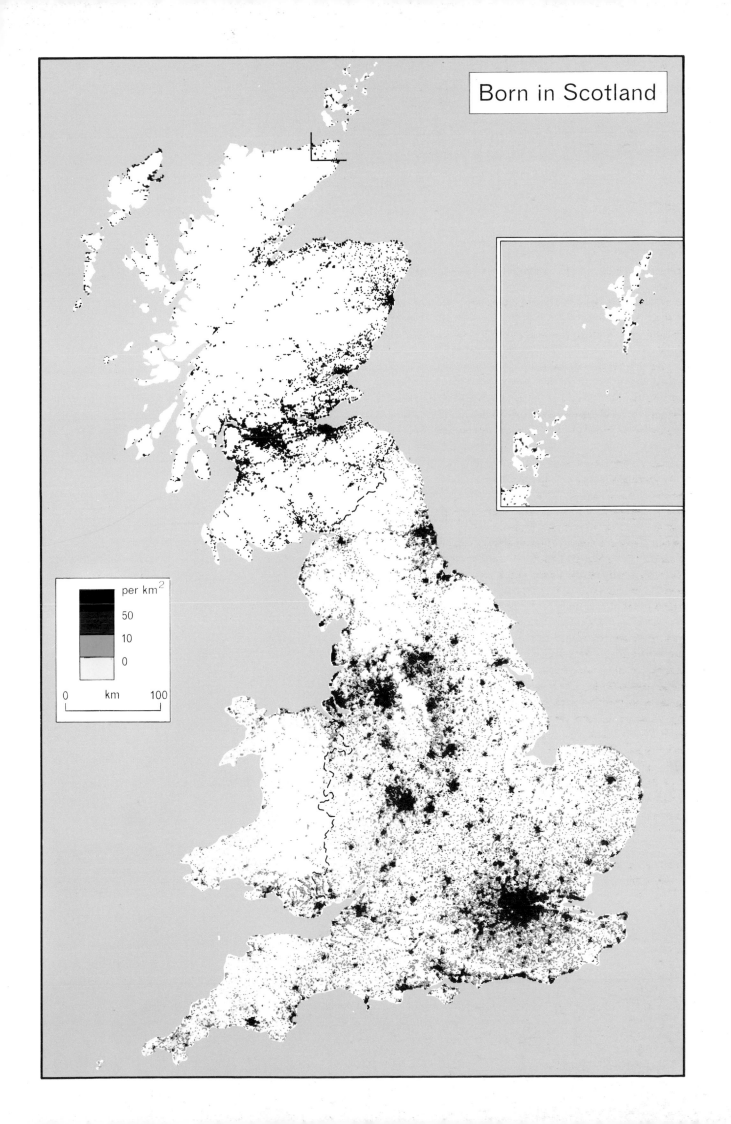

Born in Scotland

per km²

50

10

0

0   km   100

MAP 6

Born in Wales

(Absolute numbers: People born in Wales per kilometre square)

In 1971, there were 2,825,900 people born in Wales who were
living in Great Britain, 2,182,600 of them in Wales itself, 632,500
in England and only 10,800 in Scotland. The Welsh born made up
5.4 per cent of the population of Great Britain, including 82.2 per
cent of the population of Wales but only 1.4 per cent of that of
England and a mere 0.2 per cent of the population of Scotland.

There are indications that the Welsh born have settled selectively
outside Wales. Welsh migrants have penetrated rural areas along
the border and there are considerable numbers in the south Midlands and Somerset. While the low numbers of Welsh born in
some areas may be due to a low density of total population, this
does not apply in many more densely populated parts of Yorkshire, Tyneside, Teesside and eastern England in general, where
there are few Welsh born. Even fewer Welsh born have moved to
Scotland where, even in the densely populated Clydeside conurbation, there are very few one kilometre squares with more than
ten people born in Wales. Welsh born are largely absent from
Scottish rural areas.

The great majority of Welsh immigrants to England are of course
found in urban areas, with major concentrations in London, Birmingham and Coventry, Merseyside and the Bristol area. In the
case of smaller towns, Welsh born are most numerous within the
Bristol-London-Liverpool triangle. There are also considerable
numbers in south coast retirement areas.

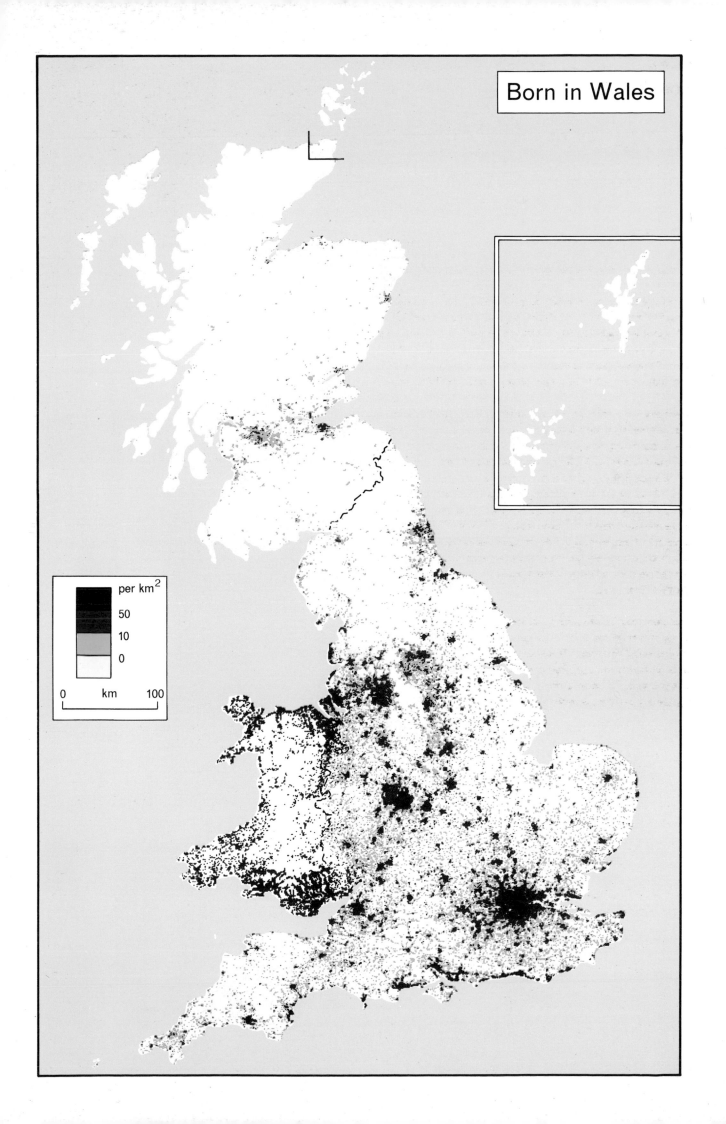

Born in Wales

per km²
50
10
0

0   km   100

MAP 7
Born in the Irish Republic

(Absolute numbers: People born in the Irish Republic per kilometre square)

The 693,400 people born in the Irish Republic represented 1.3 per cent of the total population of Great Britain. Of these 647,300 lived in England, 32,500 in Scotland and only 13,600 in Wales.

This map, unlike those of the Scots and Welsh, does not show the country of origin. It also shows a quite different pattern of cumulative migration and settlement in England; people born in the Irish Republic are more concentrated in urban areas than are the Scots and Welsh, particularly in the major conurbations of Greater London, the West Midlands, Merseyside and South East Lancashire, though many smaller towns also have significant numbers. They are relatively few in number in the north east and in Cumbria and they are very thinly spread in the rural areas of the Welsh Border, eastern England and the south west. Clusters in retirement centres are probably of young Irish workers as well as retired persons. In Scotland, people born in the Irish Republic are concentrated in Clydeside, and are relatively few in number in the rural areas.

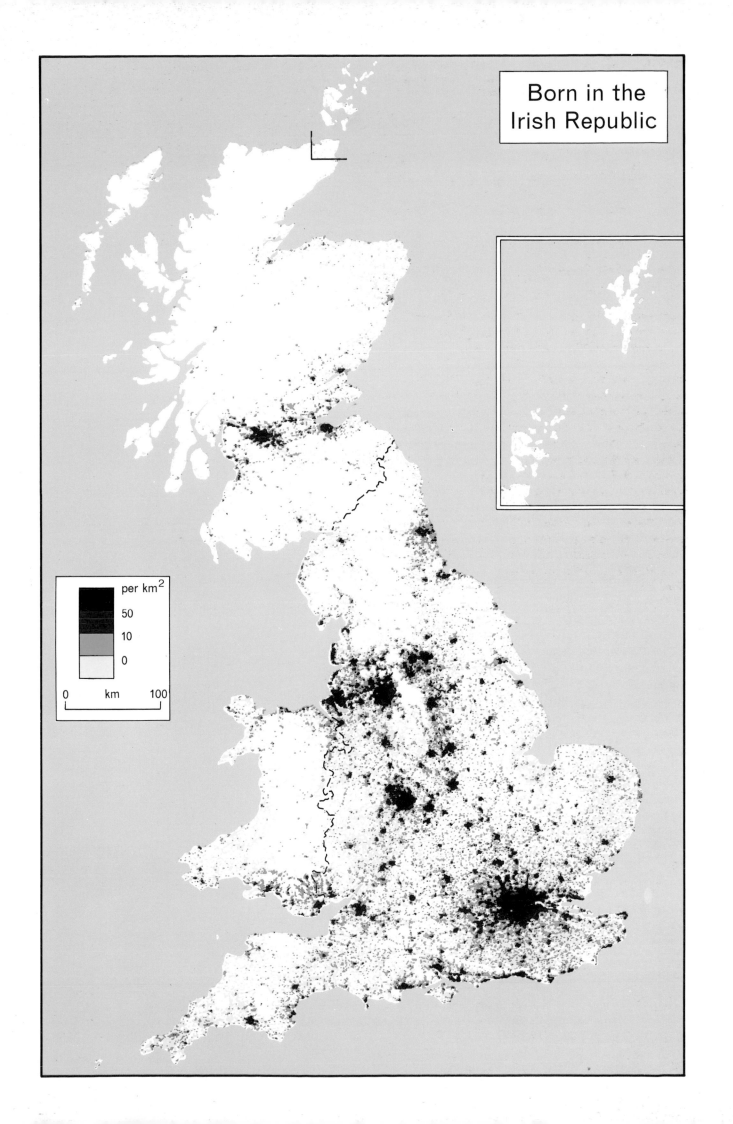

Born in the
Irish Republic

per km²
50
10
0

0   km   100

MAP 8
New Commonwealth parentage

(Absolute numbers: people with New Commonwealth parentage per kilometre square)

A census-based examination of the ethnic composition of the population must rest on country-of-birth data, which in 1971 included data on the country of birth of all present residents and on the countries of birth of their parents.

Particular interest centred on the distribution of people of New Commonwealth origin, whether born in Great Britain or not, and the SAS included summary figures for this group. The New Commonwealth comprises all countries of the Commonwealth in 1971, except Australia, Canada and New Zealand. This map shows the distribution, in absolute numbers per square kilometre, of the totals of people:

i   born in Great Britain with both parents born in the New
    Commonwealth;
ii born in the New Commonwealth with both parents born in the
    New Commonwealth;
iii born in the New Commonwealth with one parent born in the
    New Commonwealth.

Such individuals, in 1971, numbered about $1\frac{1}{4}$ million (2.3 per cent of the total population of Great Britain), of whom about 917,600 (1.7 per cent) were New Commonwealth immigrants in the strict sense of the word, having been born in the New Commonwealth with at least one parent also born there.

People of New Commonwealth parentage were very unevenly distributed, comprising 4.3 per cent of the population in south east England and 4.1 per cent in the West Midlands, but only 0.4 per cent in northern England and in Wales and 0.3 per cent in Scotland.

They were found almost wholly in urban areas. The lowest category (yellow) indicates squares with 25 or more people but none of New Commonwealth origin and covers the great bulk of rural areas throughout the country. Zero or low values, however, are not confined to such thinly settled districts; they also occur in major suburban zones, as for example around London, south of Manchester and in the Wirral peninsula. Values are also generally low in coalfield/industrial areas, becoming increasingly so towards the north.

The largest continuous areas of high value squares are in London and the West Midlands, but at least a few such squares occur in every large and medium sized town, especially in the axial belt between London, Liverpool and Leeds.

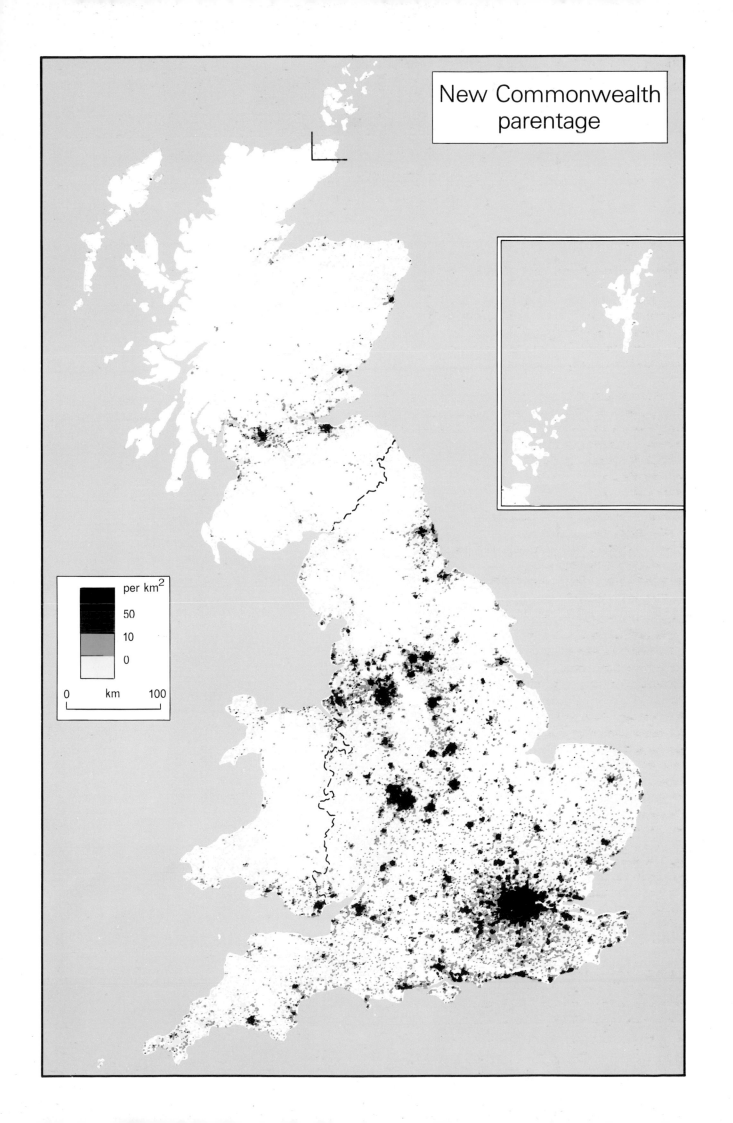

New Commonwealth
parentage

per km²
50
10
0

0   km   100

MAP 9
Sex composition

(Signed chi-square)

As well as showing the distribution of total population, the maps in this atlas portray the spatial patterns of a variety of characteristics of the British population such as age, occupation, birthplace, housing conditions, educational attainment and, in this case, sex. Of these, only data on sex are available for every inhabited square, so that the general appearance of this map, where every populated square is coloured, is very different from the rest.

Since the two sexes tend to live together in family groups, their individual distributions are generally similar. Such contrasts as do occur reflect a variety of influences. The preponderance of male births among the population as a whole and the fact that women generally live longer than men gives some correlation with fertility and age structure: males are present in higher proportions where there are large numbers of children, while females are most numerous where the population has a high proportion of elderly people. In addition, migration movements, which are commonly sex-selective, can influence sex composition in several different ways, by deducting from or adding to the number of males or females in a particular area.

This map shows where there are concentrations or deficiencies of males. In Great Britain as a whole, in 1971, males formed 48.5 per cent of the total population. Because such a high proportion of the populated squares have values quite close to this national average, the map is designed to identify the two extremes. Thus it is different from all other maps in this atlas in having only three classes, a fact reflected in the use of a different colour scheme where green denotes concentrations of males, brick-red denotes deficiencies of males (or concentrations of females), and the intervening, near average squares are coloured yellow.

At the regional level, deviations from the mean are very small and the major contrasts are between or within individual settlements. Areas with concentrations of males (green) tend to be small and scattered, occurring mainly in heavily industrialised areas such as the West Midlands, South Yorkshire, the area of Slough and Staines, Teesside and in pockets on the coalfields; some inner city areas, mainly in the Midlands and the south, also have significant concentrations of males. The presence of certain New Commonwealth immigrant groups among whom males predominated is likely to have had an effect on some of these areas. Concentrations of males are also common in rural areas, usually because women leave such areas in greater numbers than men, possibly because of inadequate female employment opportunities.

Deficiency of males (shown as brick-red squares) is most marked in coastal retirement areas. The coasts of north Kent, Sussex, Hampshire, Dorset, Devon, North Wales and west Lancashire (Southport, Blackpool, Morecambe) stand out clearly on the map. In several older urban areas, notably west London, Liverpool, Newcastle and the Scottish cities, there are deficiencies of males which may be due to the selective in-migration of younger women, the out-migration of men and, in some cases, higher male mortality rates in deprived areas. There are no such cases, however, in the cities of the English Midlands. The few areas with deficiencies of males are largely confined to market towns, inland spas and other retirement centres.

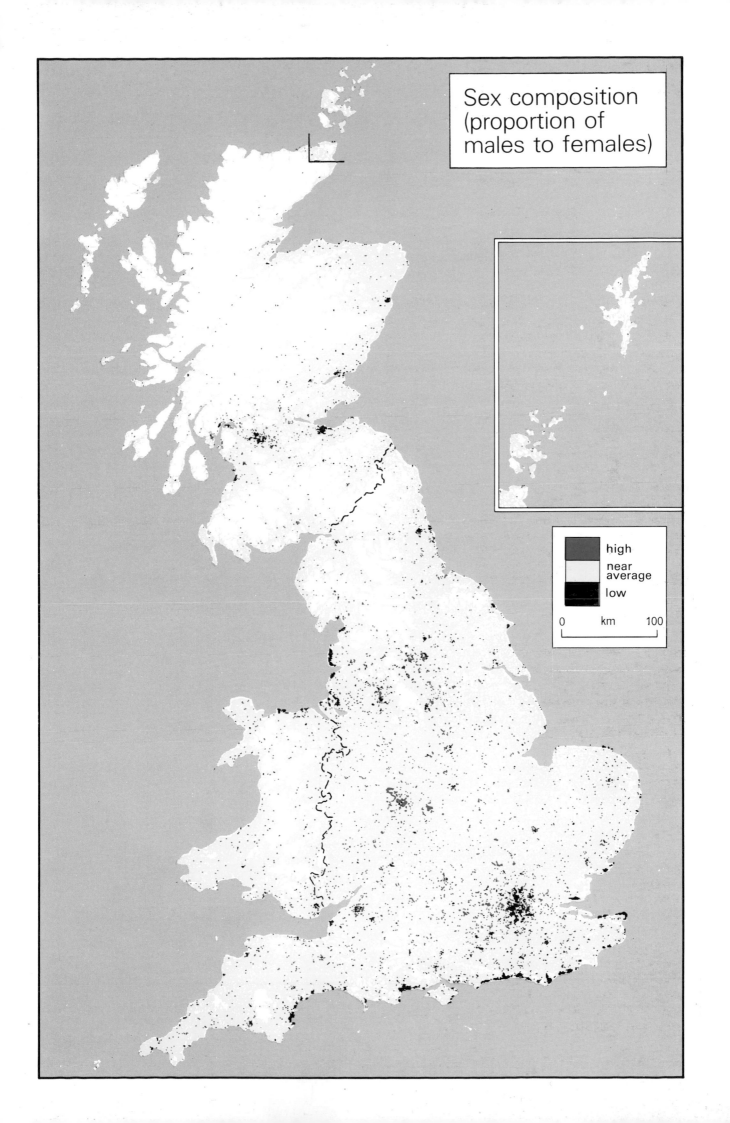

Sex composition
(proportion of
males to females)

high
near
average
low

0   km   100

MAP 10
Fertility of young married women

(Signed chi-square)

Most births are to women aged 16–29 and hence this age-group gives an indication, albeit incomplete, of regional variations in fertility. The map is based on the numbers of children ever born in marriage to currently married women aged 16–29 living in private households at the time of the Census. In 1971, nationally there were 1200 children per 1000 such women and differences between Standard Regions were quite small, values ranging from 1110 in the South East to 1280 in the North West. In Scotland the value was 1320 per 1000.

The map reveals a preponderance of below average (yellow) and low (red) values in the south and east of Great Britain, while above average (blue) and high (purple) squares predominate in the west and north, the distinction being essentially one between the 'Highland' and 'Lowland' zones.

Looking at the map in more detail, areas of high values are most extensive in the conubations of the Midlands and north – for example in Clydeside, Tyneside, Teesside, West Yorkshire, South East Lancashire, Merseyside, the West Midlands and Coventry. Such concentrations are rare in the south and east, the biggest occurring in the east end of London. In many cities, high values are particularly frequent in suburbs and urban fringes where there is newer housing, enclosing areas of mainly low values (red) in city centres; this is visible, for example, in Aberdeen, Edinburgh, Hull, Bristol and Plymouth. In most of the older coalfield industrial areas, for example in County Durham and South Wales, blue rather than purple squares predominate.

Most of inner and suburban London stands out as a distinctive area of mainly low values, speckled with below average values, which become predominant in the commuter belt. Outside London, red areas are much smaller and more dispersed, occurring mainly in non-industrial districts, for example in west Edinburgh, Brighton, York, Norwich, Cambridge, Oxford and Torbay.

Apart from the broad regional variations already mentioned, the patterns on this map are associated with those of social class and economic activity shown on Maps 15–20.

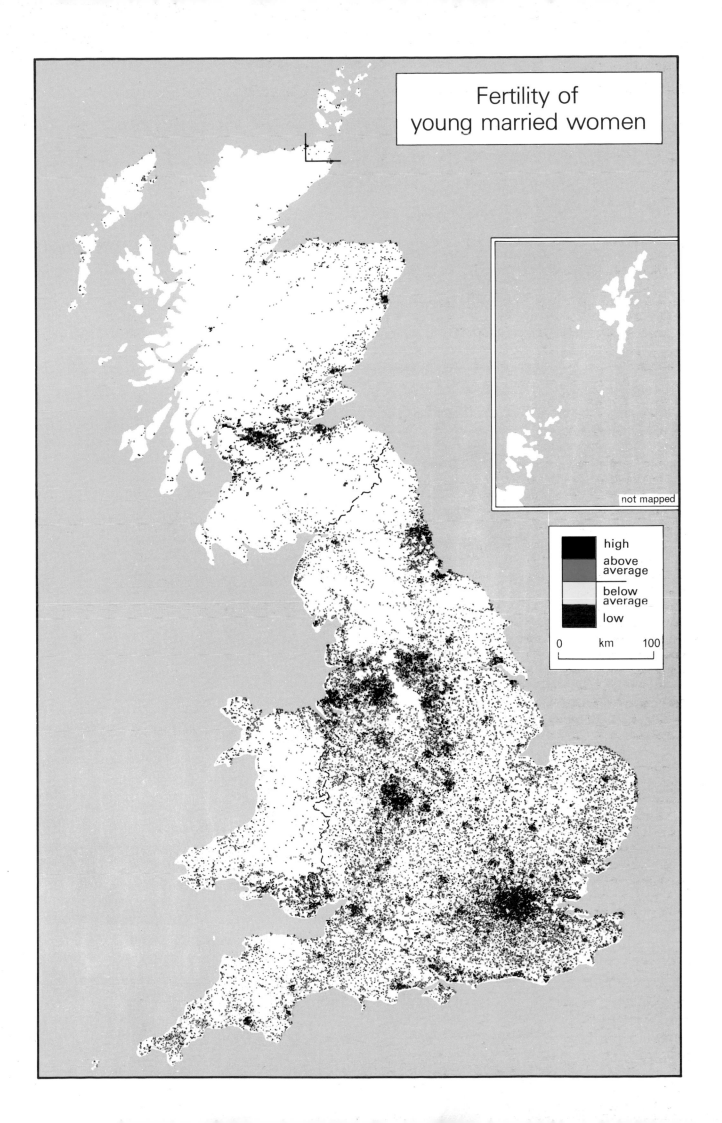

Fertility of
young married women

not mapped

high
above average
below average
low

0   km   100

MAP 11
Children

(Signed chi-square)

Children under 15 years of age formed 24 per cent of the total
population in 1971 and their distribution owes more to the distribution of younger married couples than to regional or class variations in fertility which, nowadays, are relatively slight. Thus the
patterns on the map of children come close to being a mirror
image of those on the map of persons above the age of retirement. Almost all the areas with concentrations of elderly people
have deficiencies of children. Children are especially concentrated
in the suburban rings around many large and small cities, and in
the New Towns, where there are new housing estates inhabited
mainly by young married couples. Parts of the country where children are particularly numerous include Clydeside, Teesside, south
and east Lancashire, much of the West Midlands and a zone to
the immediate west of London. Smaller urban areas which appear
particularly youthful include Grimsby, Gloucester and Coventry and
small Midland towns such as Daventry, Banbury, Bicester and
Leighton Buzzard.

The largest area with a deficiency of children is Greater London
(though the East End is an exception), and this phenomenon can
be seen on a smaller scale in the other conurbation cores, though
small pockets of high values, often associated with slum clearance and the rebuilding of housing, also occur in such areas.
Coastal resorts, together with many deeply rural areas, tend to
have a deficiency of children, essentially because young adults
tend to migrate to areas with greater employment opportunities,
leaving relatively few people of child bearing age.

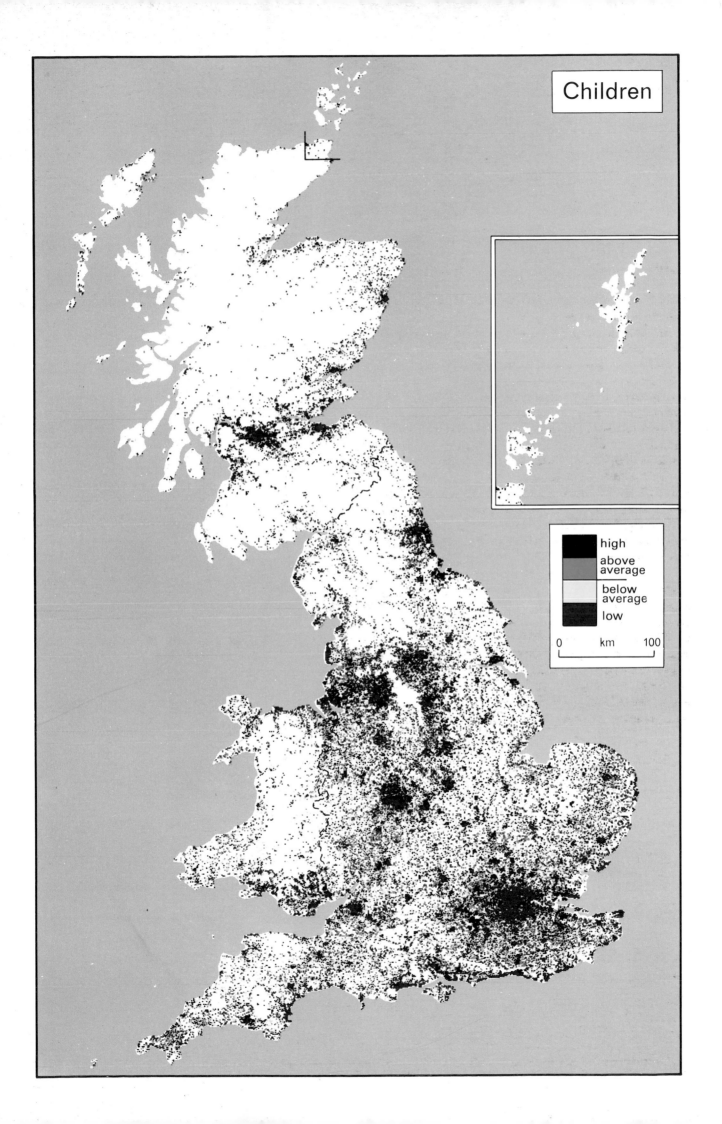

Children

MAP 12
Persons over retirement age

(Signed chi-square)

This map shows the distribution of people beyond the age of retirement (65 years for men, 60 years for women), who accounted for 16 per cent of the total population of Great Britain in 1971. Owing to the long-term ageing of the British population, which results from reduced fertility and increased longevity, this group continues to grow both in absolute numbers and as a proportion of the total. Its distribution helps to pick out those areas where social provision for the aged is particularly necessary.

Concentration along the coastlines is particularly marked, with a near-continuous belt of high values along the southern and south-western coasts of England reflecting the popularity of these districts as retirement areas. Similar belts can be seen in North Wales, west Lancashire and parts of the east coast. Many inland resorts (Windermere, Keswick, Harrogate), spas (Bath, Malvern, Leamington), cathedral cities (York, Salisbury, Winchester) and market towns fall into the same category. Many rural areas also have concentrations of elderly people; in this case the phenomenon is due mainly to the out-migration of the younger age-groups, though some rural areas of high amenity value, such as the Weald, the Cotswolds, Dorset, Somerset and Devon, are retirement areas.

The distribution pattern of elderly people in major urban areas is complex. Most of the older urban areas, including the inner suburbs, have ageing populations, but some inner conurbation districts have mainly young bedsitter populations. In the case of Liverpool, for example, the city core is an area of low values; a ring including Crosby, the Queen's Drive area, Birkenhead and Wallasey, has high values; beyond this a third zone, mainly of new housing estates, largely council-owned, is essentially youthful; and finally an outer ring, including Heswall, Hoylake and Southport, which are also retirement areas, again has high values. London has a similar concentric zoning but the rings are displaced by a central area (the West End) of prosperous older people which has forced the bedsitter belt outwards to Earl's Court to the west and New Cross to the south-east, beyond which the ageing inner suburbs are clearly visible. Newer housing areas, including several New Towns, which lack elderly people, form a fourth ring, and the outermost retirement zone is almost entirely confined to the south, in the Weald and on the coast.

There are also pronounced differences between conurbations. The West Midlands has relatively few squares with concentrations of elderly people and a large area in which the population is generally youthful. The South East Lancashire and West Yorkshire conurbations have very complicated patterns with numerous concentrations of elderly people in the core areas of their constituent settlements and youthful population in the intervening, more recently developed, areas; north east England and the Scottish cities particularly Clydeside, show a similar pattern.

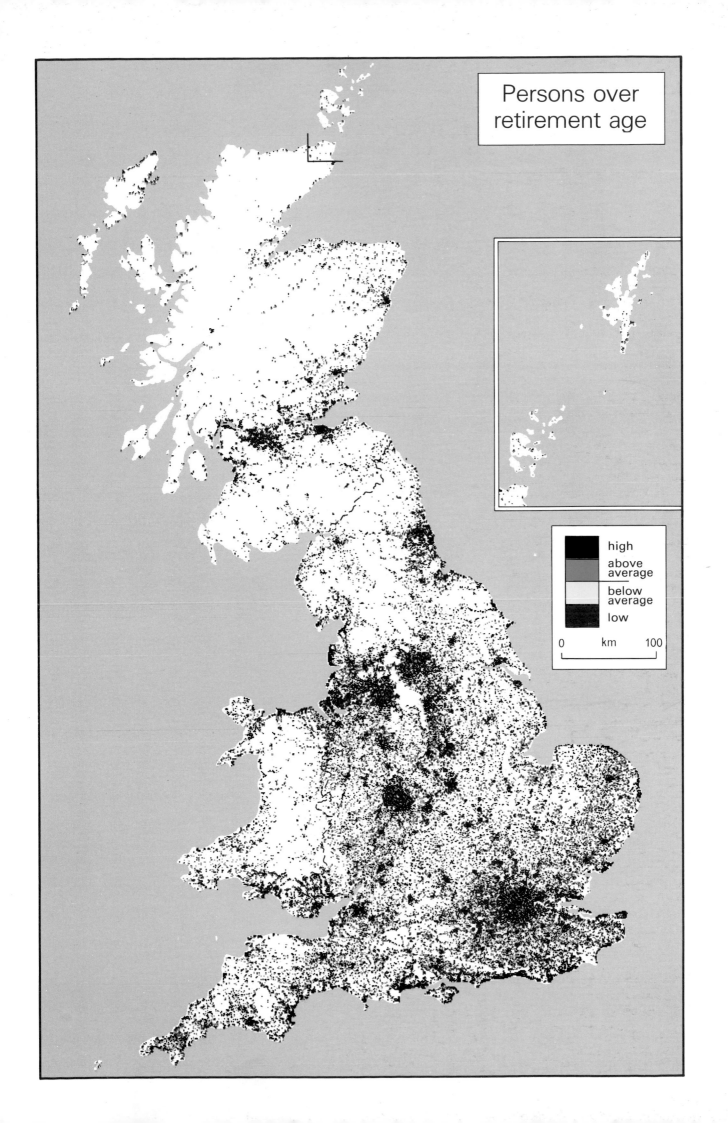

Persons over retirement age

high
above average
below average
low

0 km 100

MAP 13
Types of age structure

(Signed chi-square)

The map presented here is to some degree experimental in that it attempts, by using data on several age-groups, to illustrate spatial variations in the total age structure of the population of Great Britain. The other maps in this atlas portray the spatial distribution of a single characteristic of people or households and include two age-based maps, *Children* (Map 11) and *Persons over retirement age* (Map 12), chosen from among the many different age-groups identified in the Census.

The number of possible classes on a map of total age structure depends on the number of age-groups used in its compilation and it was decided to restrict the latter to the three most commonly used in demographic analyses: age-groups 0–14 (children), 15–64 (adults) and 65 and over (elderly), distinguishing in each case those squares where the values of one or more of the three groups were in the high category based on the chi-squared criterion (see Introduction, page 6 and Appendix 2). The seven types of age structure and the number of squares of each type were:

| Type | Colour | Age-groups | | | Number of | Percentage |
		0–14	15–64	65 and over	squares	of total
A	Blue	−	−	+	10,084	14.9
B	Green	−	+	+	5,079	7.5
C	Purple	−	+	−	3,549	5.3
D	Red	+	+	−	4,775	7.1
E	Brick red	+	−	−	7,007	10.4
F	Brown	+	−	+	2,222	3.3
G	Yellow	−	−	−	34,759	51.5

Key + in the high category − in other categories

Type A (blue): high values for the elderly. This type shows the most distinctive distribution and covers many of the districts already identified (Map 12) as retirement areas. The coastal resort distribution is particularly striking with blue areas in and around Morecambe, Blackpool, Southport and Scarborough, along the North Wales coast and, above all, in a near continuous strip along the south coast from Devon to Kent. Inland squares in this category are much less numerous, occurring in small pockets in inland resorts, spas and cathedral cities, especially in the southern counties. Upland rural areas also have a scatter of blue squares; while in many cases retirement is an obvious reason, in more remote districts the out-migration of adults is a likely cause of a high proportion of elderly.

Type B (green): high values for both adults and the elderly. Although these areas, too, have high values for those aged 65 and over, in this case there are also high values for the adult (15–64) age-groups and the spatial distribution of Type B areas is very different from that of Type A. In many cases, the populations of Type B areas include a high proportion of middle-aged whose offspring no longer live with them so that the proportion of children is very low, but it is also common, particularly in London and the Midlands, to find a high proportion of young adults, especially students and recent in-migrants. Type B is particularly characteristic of inner suburban areas; the biggest block of such squares is in London. Central Edinburgh is also striking (and contrasts with Glasgow) and there are pockets in Newcastle, Manchester, Bristol and Plymouth. The phenomenon is repeated in the majority of towns, both large and small, including some commuter areas, for example south west of London.

Type C (purple): high values for adults. Since older adults are commonly found in association with the elderly and younger adults with their children, this type, in which only the value for adults is high, is less extensive and most commonly occurs in close juxtaposition to Type B. It is thus found mainly in inner suburbs, for example in London and the West Midlands, but also extends into the outer suburban fringes. It is much less common in Scotland and northern England than in the Midlands and south of England, probably because of long continued movement of adults from the former to the latter.

Type D (red): high values for both adults and children, and *Type E (brick red): high values for children only* generally occur in association with each other in outer suburban and commuter rings around the cities. This is most clearly marked around the West Midland conurbation, and especially London where central green and purple zones give way outwards first to red and then to brick red areas. The latter, which are considerably more extensive, include the most recently developed areas where young families predominate and thus the proportion of children in the population is particularly high. Detailed examination of the map reveals similar red/brick red zones on the outskirts of most established urban centres, large and small. Entirely new developments, however, as to the south west of London or in the most recent New Towns, lack this core/periphery contrast and are wholly brick red. The Midlands and South contrast with Scotland and the North; in the latter, brick red squares are much more numerous than red, indicating the combined effects of relatively high fertility (see Map 10) and the out-migration of adults.

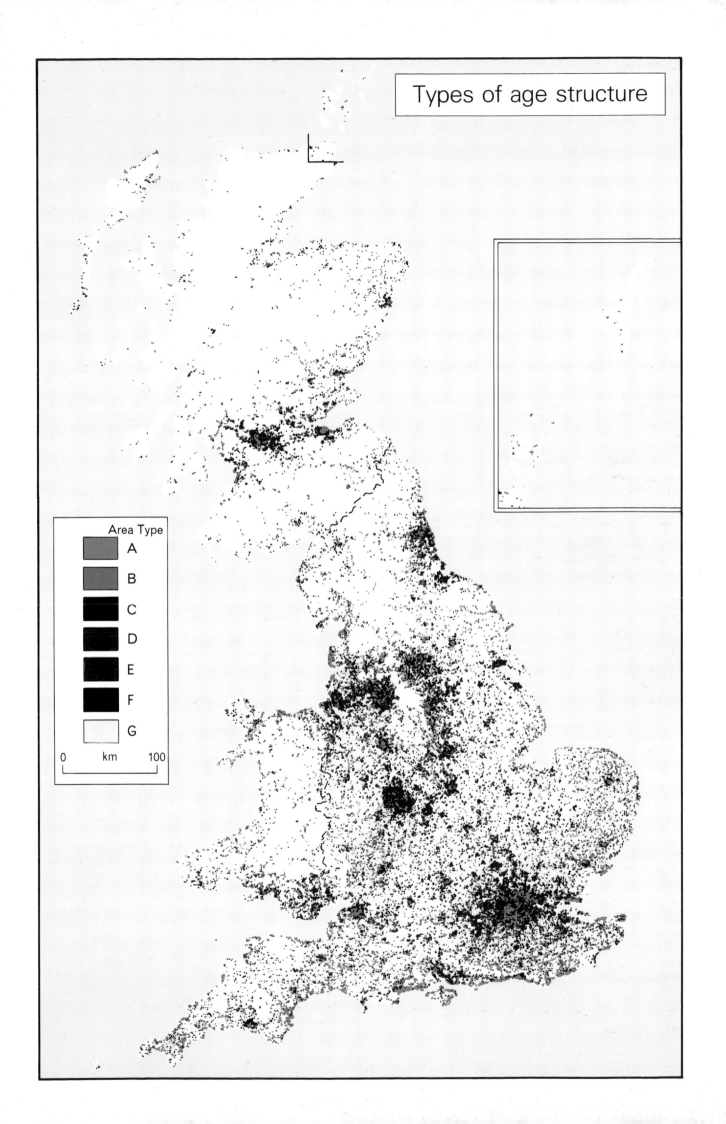

Types of age structure

Area Type

A
B
C
D
E
F
G

0   km   100

MAP 14
Educational qualifications

Type F (brown): high values for both children and the elderly is the rarest category. It is difficult to suggest a mechanism by which this combination might be produced other than juxtapositions within individual squares of smaller areas with high proportions of children or of elderly people in their populations. Such juxtatpositions would occur, for example, where special housing, sheltered housing, or institutes for the elderly were built as part of new housing developments.

Type G (yellow): no group in the high category is the most widespread, covering rather more than half the squares on the map. In terms of population, however, it is much less significant, since it occurs for the most part in the more thinly populated rural and semi-rural areas and is virtually absent from densely populated urban districts.

All-in-all, the map graphically illustrates the way in which the British population is spatially sorted by age, which is in turn linked to many other characteristics. Different age-groups not only have different life-styles but live in different areas as well, and the individual's life cycle very often involves migration from one of these areal types to another.

(Signed chi-square)

The 10 per cent SAS provide information on the number of people in employment who have school-leaving standard qualifications equivalent to GCE A level (11 per cent of those employed) and on the number of people in employment who have degree or equivalent qualifications (9 per cent of those employed). Many people who have degree-level qualifications also have school-leaving qualifications and the two groups were added together in order to weight the map towards emphasising those areas where these groups are particularly concentrated. The result is a particularly distinctive pattern.

Areas with high values for the educationally qualified are particularly widespread in the London region, especially in the western and southern suburbs, both inner and outer; there is a sharp dividing line in north London, for example, between Hampstead and Camden, continuing northward to New Barnet. Elsewhere in England, relatively small suburban areas have concentrations of qualified people, notably in the south of the South East Lancashire conurbation, on the west side of the Wirral peninsula and the north of Bristol. University quarters can be picked out, as in the Edgbaston district of Birmingham, south Liverpool and Cottingham (near Hull), along with University towns such as Cambridge, Durham, Oxford and St Andrews. The great majority of Scottish areas are above the British average, the only major exceptions being parts of Glasgow and the Fife coalfield; like Wales, however, Scotland lost many of its better qualified sons and daughters by emigration to England (Map 5) or abroad.

Areas with low values for qualified workers include the coalfields of England and Wales, the East End of London, the conurbations of the Midlands and North and many rural areas, especially in East Anglia and the south west.

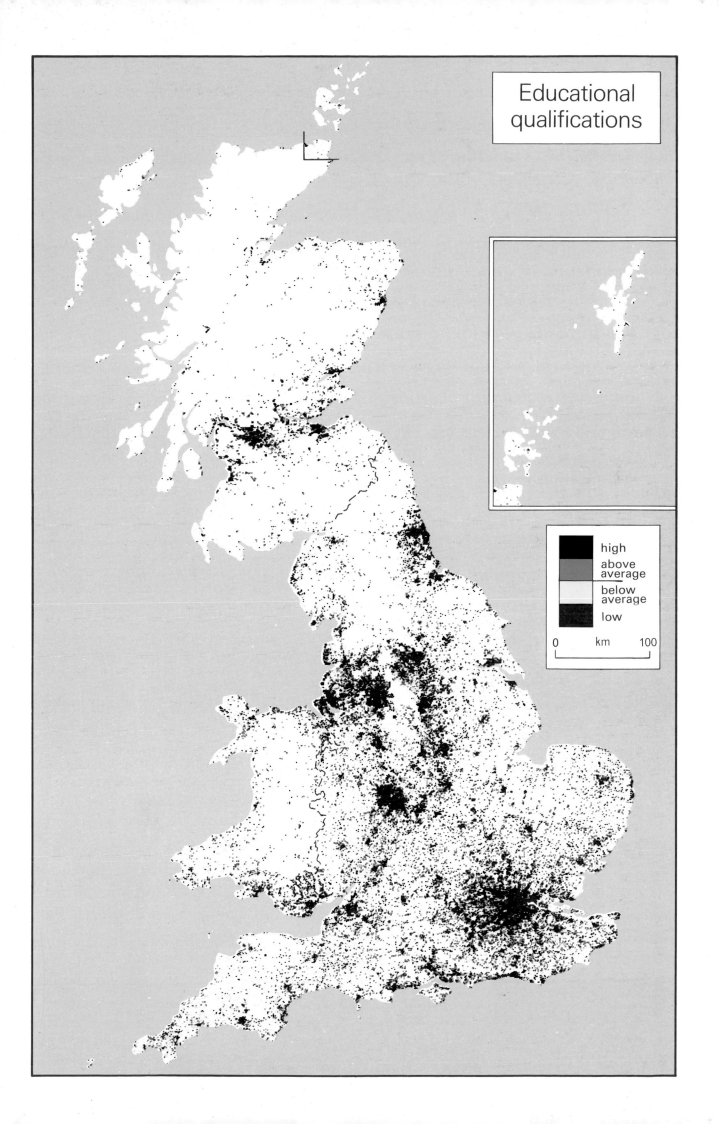

Educational
qualifications

high
above
average
below
average
low

0   km   100

MAP 15
Foremen and skilled manual workers

(Signed chi-square)

This map shows where the socio-economic groups of foremen and skilled manual workers lived. These groups (socio-economic groups 8 and 9) constituted 24.6 per cent of the working population and show particularly strong regional contrasts.

The socio-economic groups used in the Census are derived from the combination of data on the individual's industry, occupation and employment status. There is an arbitrary element in the definition of the groups, and their distributional patterns can be affected by the way in which definitions are applied; for example, farm workers are excluded from the skilled category because of the range of skilled and less skilled work which they perform. Nevertheless, the overall patterns are revealing and significant.

Particularly striking on this map is the marked dichotomy between the below average and low values for foremen and skilled manual workers in much of southern and south eastern England, and the strong concentrations of above average and high values in the coalfields and industrial conurbations of Yorkshire, Derbyshire, Nottinghamshire, the Black Country, the Potteries, north east England, the Midlands, South Wales and the Scottish lowlands (except for the wealthier sections of Edinburgh and Glasgow).

Within south eastern England, high values for foremen and skilled manual workers are found in much smaller pockets: in Northamptonshire, Norwich and Ipswich, along the Thames and Medway estuaries, in Luton, High Wycombe, Hounslow and Southampton. In the south west, Plymouth, Swindon, the Radstock coalfield and south and east Bristol have clear concentrations. In South Wales, above average and high values on the coalfied contrast with areas of low values in Swansea and Cardiff, while in north west England, the Lancashire coalfield, north east Lancashire and north east Manchester contrast with low values in south Manchester, the coastal resorts and parts of Liverpool. West Cumbria, Teesside and Scunthorpe also stand out as areas with high values for foremen and skilled manual workers. Rural areas are notable for having rather more below average than above average values, partly through the exclusion of farm workers from the skilled category.

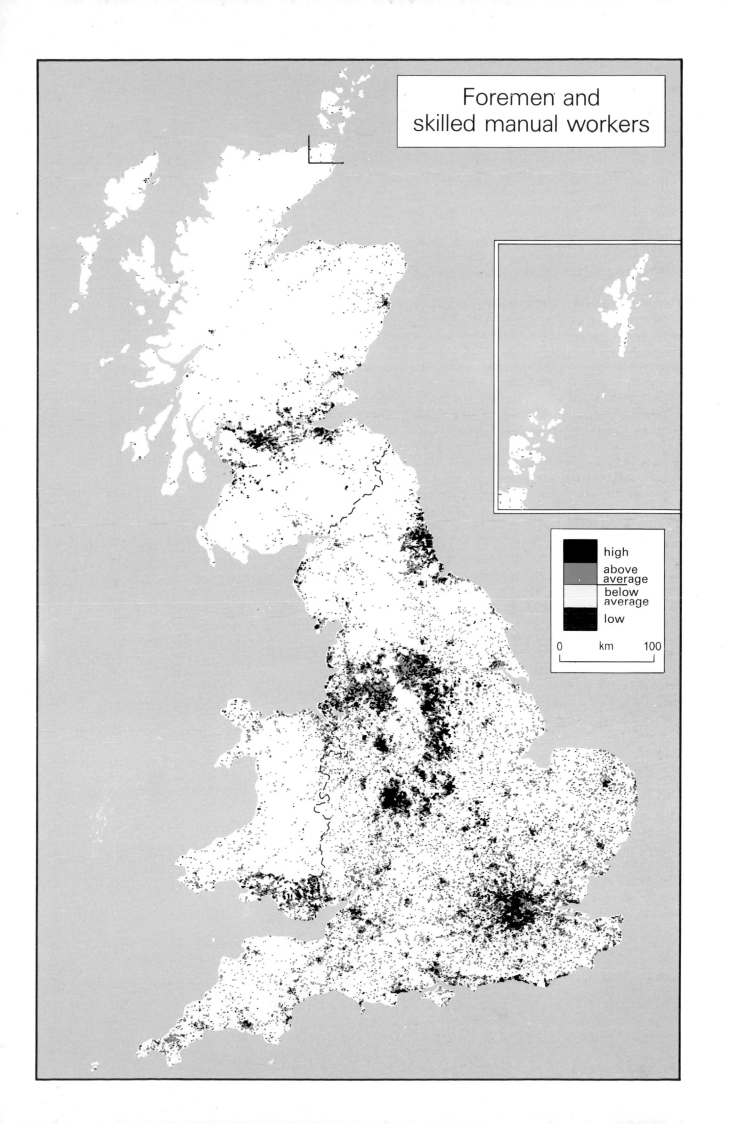

Foremen and
skilled manual workers

high
above average
below average
low

0   km   100

MAP 16
Unskilled manual workers

(Signed chi-square)

This map shows where the socio-economic group of unskilled manual workers lived. Such workers (socio-economic group 11) are a diminishing sector of the labour force who, in 1971, accounted for only 7.8 per cent of the working population. Above-average and high values are frequent in heavy industrial and coalfield areas. As a result, while there is a complex pattern of high and low values in each region, the most obvious contrast is between the south and east, with frequent below average and low values, and the rest of the country.

Nevertheless, the largest continuous area of grid squares with high values for unskilled workers is found in central London and the East End. Moreover, each conurbation core has a small nucleus of this sort and the same feature can be seen in the majority of smaller urban centres. There is some association with council housing, since the poorer sections of the community can call on such accommodation as long as their place of residence (on a Local Authority basis) is stable. Low values for unskilled workers are characteristic of prosperous suburbs such as south Manchester, north Leeds, south west Sheffield, or north Newcastle, large parts of London, western Edinburgh and coastal resort areas. In addition, the majority of rural areas have below average values for unskilled manual workers.

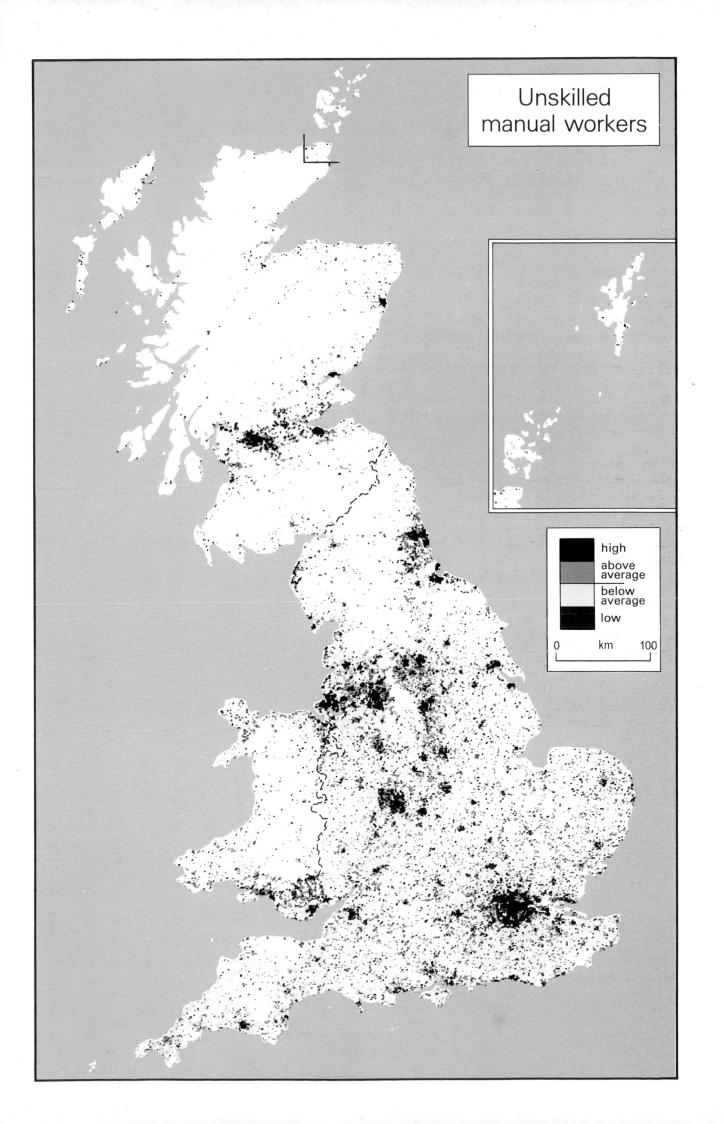

Unskilled
manual workers

high

above
average

below
average

low

0   km   100

MAP 17
Farmers, foresters and fishermen

(Absolute numbers: number of farmers, foresters and fishermen per kilometre square)

This map shows where workers in the agricultural sector of industry lived. The Small Area Statistics on which the map is based group people in employment into only seven categories, rather than the 27 of the Standard Industrial Classification used in the published Census volumes. Consequently, the workers mapped here include those employed in forestry and fishing as well as in agriculture proper, though farmers and farm workers make up some 95 per cent of the total.

In 1971, approximately 640,000 people were employed in the agricultural sector, forming 2.7 per cent of the working population of Great Britain. Regional variations were considerable, from a maximum of 8.6 per cent in East Anglia to only 1.2 per cent in north west England. Scotland and Wales both had over 4 per cent in this category, compared with only 2.3 per cent in England.

Since this map shows absolute numbers, it is in fact a density map which, to a large degree, reflects variations in the productivity of Britain's agricultural land, the type of agricultural activity carried out on it and, to some extent, where workers in the industry lived in clusters. Because this map, like Map 18 *Miners,* is based on the 10 per cent sample data, values of 10, 20, 30 and 40 per square are estimates derived from counts of 1, 2, 3 and 4 respectively in the 10 per cent sample. Squares are yellow where there are no agricultural workers in the 10 per cent sample, in contrast to other absolute numbers maps derived from the 100 per cent statistics, where a yellow square means 'none in that square'. The lowest category (yellow) for the most part picks out the urban fabric. Many urban areas do, however, contain a few squares with some workers called agricultural, but who are probably engaged in gardening or horticulture. Low densities (1-10 agricultural workers per sq km) are widespread throughout lowland England and the much more limited agricultural districts of Scotland and Wales. Relatively high values (red and black squares) are less numerous and more concentrated. Most of these are in lowland England, where some of the highest densities are associated with intensive fruit and vegetable production, as in the Lea Valley, north Kent, the Vale of Evesham, south west Sussex and the Fens.

Concentrations of fishermen give high densities in fishing ports. Peterhead, Aberdeen, South Shields, Fleetwood, Hull, Grimsby, Lowestoft and even Brixham are clearly visible. In a few places in upland Britain there are minor concentrations associated with large scale forestry activities.

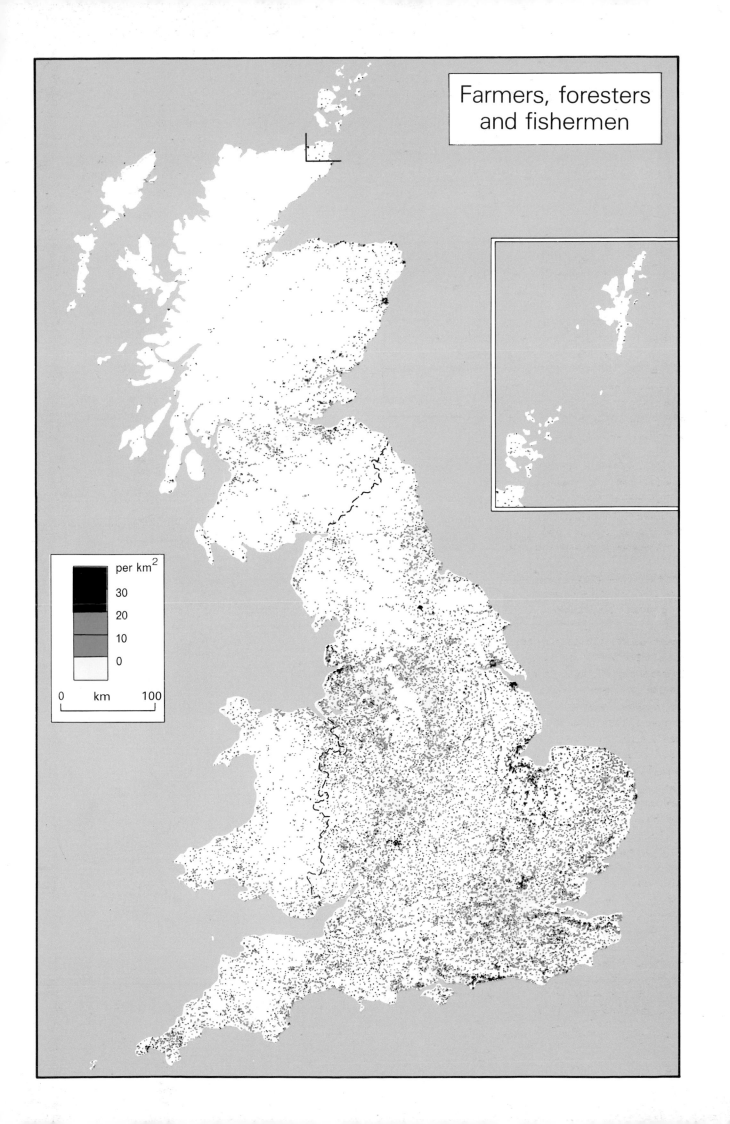

Farmers, foresters and fishermen

per km²
30
20
10
0

0   km   100

MAP 18
Miners

(Absolute numbers: number of miners and quarrymen per kilometre square)

This map shows where people working in the mining and quarrying industries lived. Workers in the coal mining industry were in the overwhelming majority among the 399,000 people in this group of industries, who constituted 1.7 per cent of the working population. That mining and quarrying now employ fewer workers than agriculture reflects the massive post-war contraction of the coal mining industry, though output has fallen less rapidly than employment, owing to increased productivity.

Workers in this sector are highly concentrated in the areas of mineral extraction and there are large regional variations: miners and quarrymen constitute between four and five per cent of those employed in the Northern region, Yorkshire/Humberside, the East Midlands and Wales, but only about 0.2 per cent in East Anglia and the South East region.

This map picks out all the coalfield areas, including such small-scale producers as Kent and Flint as well as the more important ones. It is noticeable that workers in the mining industry are still found on the older, exhausted parts of the coalfields, as in west Derbyshire and north west Durham, as well as around the active mines. The influence of other forms of mineral extraction, as for example around St Austell in Cornwall and Scunthorpe in Lincolnshire, can also be seen, as can the extensive limestone quarrying areas of Derbyshire.

The occurrence of people working in the mining and quarrying industries away from the main areas of mineral extraction is explained by such wide-spread activities as sand and gravel working and by the fact that administrative workers in these industries are included and may live in urban areas near offices located outside the mining and quarrying districts.

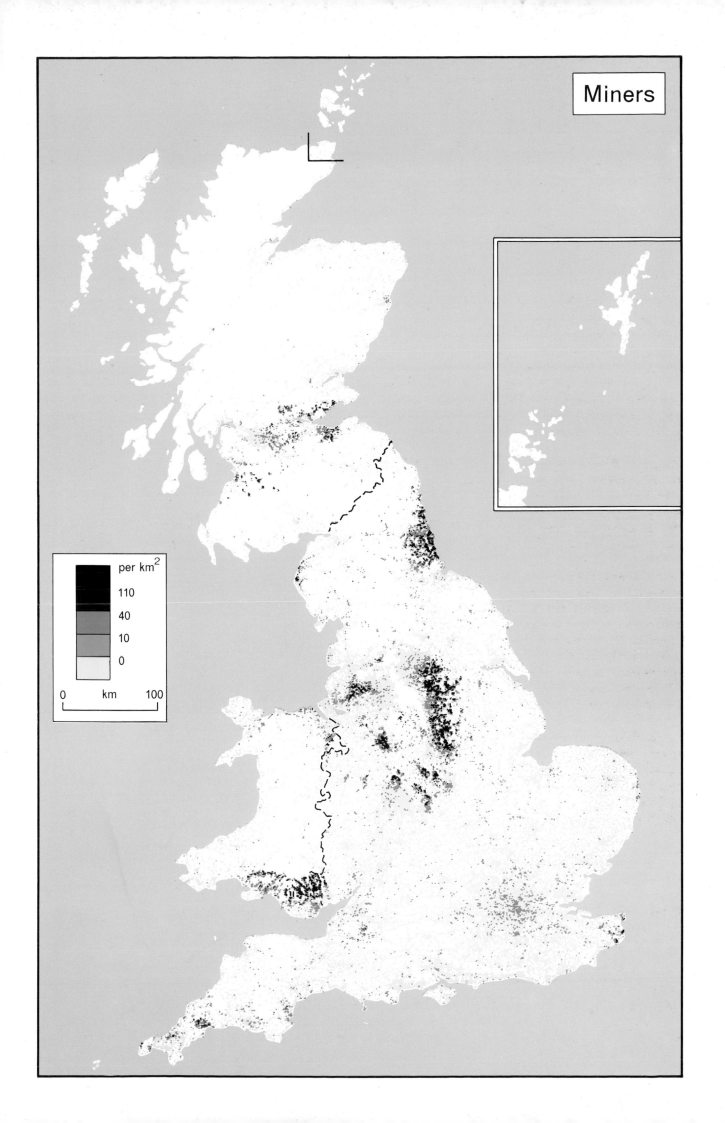

Miners

per km²
110
40
10
0

0   km   100

MAP 19
Manufacturing workers

(Signed chi-square)

In 1971, approximately eight million people, 34.5 per cent of all those in employment, were working in manufacturing industry: this map shows where such workers lived. Areas with high values are almost entirely urban, though many rural areas have clusters of manufacturing workers, many of whom are likely to travel to work in nearby towns. Thus the most significant features are the contrasts among the various major urban areas and the sometimes highly complex patterns within each conurbation.

Greater London, as on the great majority of maps in this atlas, is a special case, being dominated by a large central area in which manufacturing workers are poorly represented; the great majority are employed in service activities. Concentrations of manufacturing workers are, however, to be seen in a number of clearly defined districts – in the west from Acton and Brentford through Ealing and Southall to Slough, and in the east along the banks of the Thames and up the Lea Valley to Enfield. In contrast, the other major conurbations show high values for manufacturing workers over the greater part of their areas. This is particularly so in the West Midlands, where the area of below average and low values is extremely small, and in Manchester and West Yorkshire. Other important concentrations of manufacturing workers are to be seen on the coalfields and in such centres as Tyneside, Teesside, Merseyside, Coventry, Leicester and Bristol. Smaller manufacturing towns like Scunthorpe, Swindon, Port Talbot, Ebbw Vale and Barrow are also visible. In Scotland, Clydeside (though not the central belt), Dundee and Kilmarnock can be identified.

Although the proportions of those living in rural areas who are employed in manufacturing are generally low, there are above average and high values in the Midlands, the Bristol region and the northern Home Counties, where there are many small industrial centres as well as some major ones.

In contrast, a considerable number of sizeable urban areas stand out as deficient in manufacturing workers – Aberdeen, Edinburgh, Swansea, Cardiff, Exeter, Canterbury and Cambridge for example. Particularly clearly marked are the low values in coastal resort and retirement areas, especially in England south of a line from the Severn to the Thames.

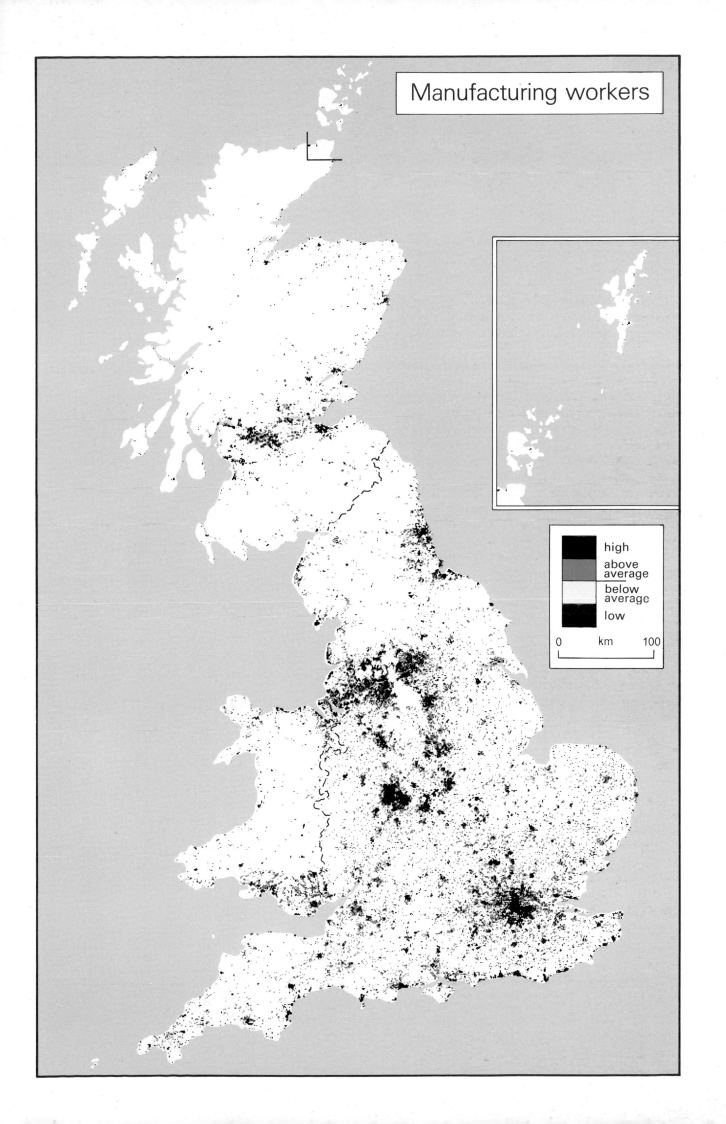

Manufacturing workers

high
above average
below average
low

0   km   100

MAP 20
Managerial and professional workers

(Signed chi-square)

This map shows where the people lived who were in the socio-economic groups embracing managerial and professional workers. This category includes all employed people in socio-economic groups 1 and 2 (employers and managers in central and local government, industry and commerce), 3 and 4 (professional workers, whether self-employed or not, engaged in work normally requiring qualifications of university degree standard) and 13 (farm employers and managers, who own, rent or manage farms employing people other than family workers). While there are, no doubt, numerous individual exceptions, the group as a whole is characterised by educational attainment and income levels both well above the national average. Professional and managerial workers thus defined made up 13.6 per cent of the working population of Great Britain in 1971, with variations from 15.3 per cent in South East England to 11–12 per cent in Northern England and Scotland.

Both regional and local variations are complex. Rural areas have a predominance of near average values and the biggest contrasts are within and between urban areas, which have most of the high and low values. Since the map shows the place of residence, not the place of work, the inner areas of cities and conurbations have low values for professional and managerial workers, such people being concentrated in the suburban fringe; but this simple pattern is often broken by local variations. In Greater London, for example, the area with low values is mainly in the east, but low values also occur in the western industrial zone. Between these two areas, a zone of high values reaches in to the West End. Otherwise, above average and high values are dominant from the Chilterns to the Channel coast. In the other conurbations, concentrations of professional and managerial workers are smaller and less continuous, becoming increasingly so towards the north. On the York-Notts-Derby coalfield, in south Lancashire, in north east England and in the Scottish lowlands, low and below average values predominate, though small concentrations of high values are visible, for example north of Leeds-Bradford, south of Teesside, in Gosforth and Whitley Bay on Tyneside, and in Edinburgh, which contrasts strongly with Glasgow in this, as in so many other respects. At the two extremes are the older coalfield areas – South Wales, Rossendale and Durham for example – and the retirement areas of the south and south west.

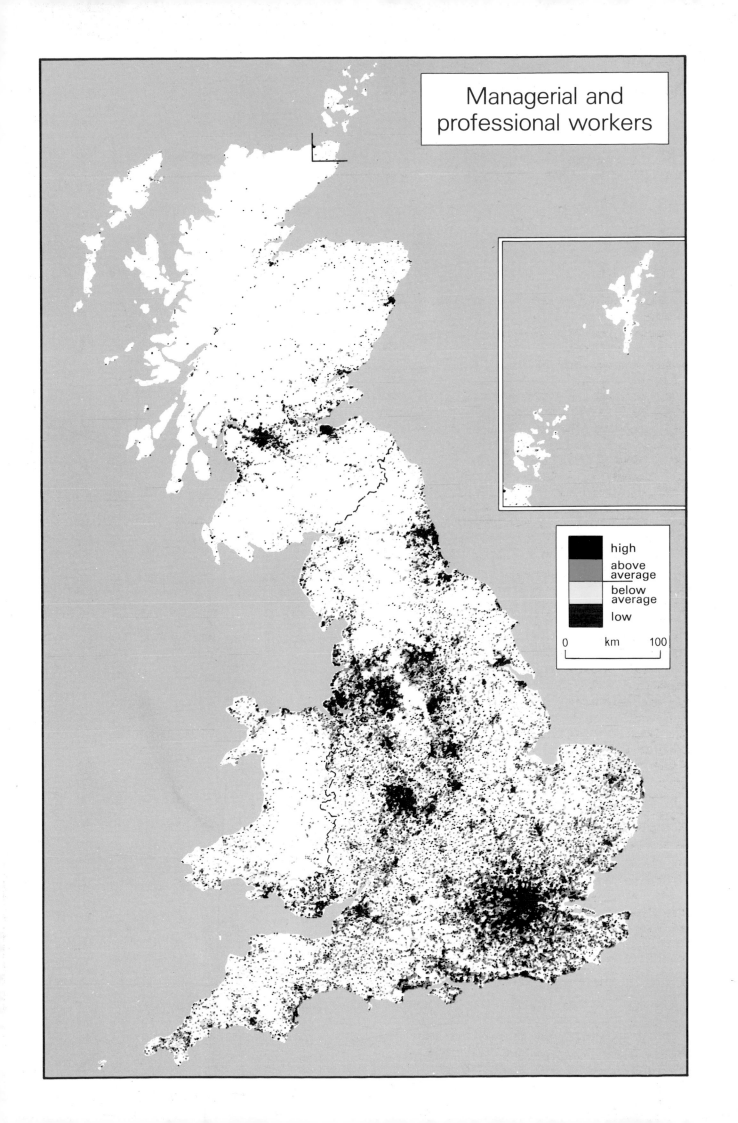

Managerial and professional workers

high
above average
below average
low

0   km   100

MAP 21
Unemployed men

(Signed chi-square)

Mapping unemployment from a decennial census presents special problems, since we know that the national and local averages have fluctuated considerably since the time of the Census; however, regional variations and the ranking of regions tend to persist, and census information is a significant indicator of relative patterns. Only unemployed men were mapped, as statistics of unemployed women are not strictly comparable.

The number unemployed in 1971 is related to the number of economically active males in the 15–64 age group; 4.2 per cent of this group were recorded as seeking work at the time of the Census. There were considerable variations in this measure, from 6.5 per cent in Scotland to only 3.1 per cent in the East Midlands.

Areas with high values for male unemployment included central Scotland (especially Clydeside), Merseyside, Humberside, north east England (particularly Tyneside and Sunderland) along with other coalfield-industrial areas such as West Yorkshire, Nottinghamshire, South Wales and West Cumbria. Concentrations of high male unemployment are also visible in other conurbations, including Manchester, Liverpool, Leeds and Bradford and even the generally much more prosperous West Midlands and London. Since the Census was held in April, well outside the summer holiday season, many coastal resorts, such as Torbay, Yarmouth, Scarborough, Blackpool, Southport and Morecambe, formed pockets of high male unemployment. Remote rural areas like the Outer Hebrides, Cornwall and the western peninsulas of Wales also show high values for unemployment.

Conversely, extensive areas of low values for male unemployment are clear in Greater London, the Midlands (especially the East Midlands) and the Bristol region, while such places as Barrow, Kendal, Carlisle, Llanelli and west Swansea stand out as bright spots in otherwise depressed areas.

This map shows a fairly close resemblance to the map of unskilled workers, since it is among this group that male unemployment is usually most severe. It also illustrates well the advantages of kilometre-square data, which not only portray the broad regional contrasts available in published statistics but also pick out local variations, identifying, for example, the problem of male unemployment in inner city areas or areas like the London dockland.

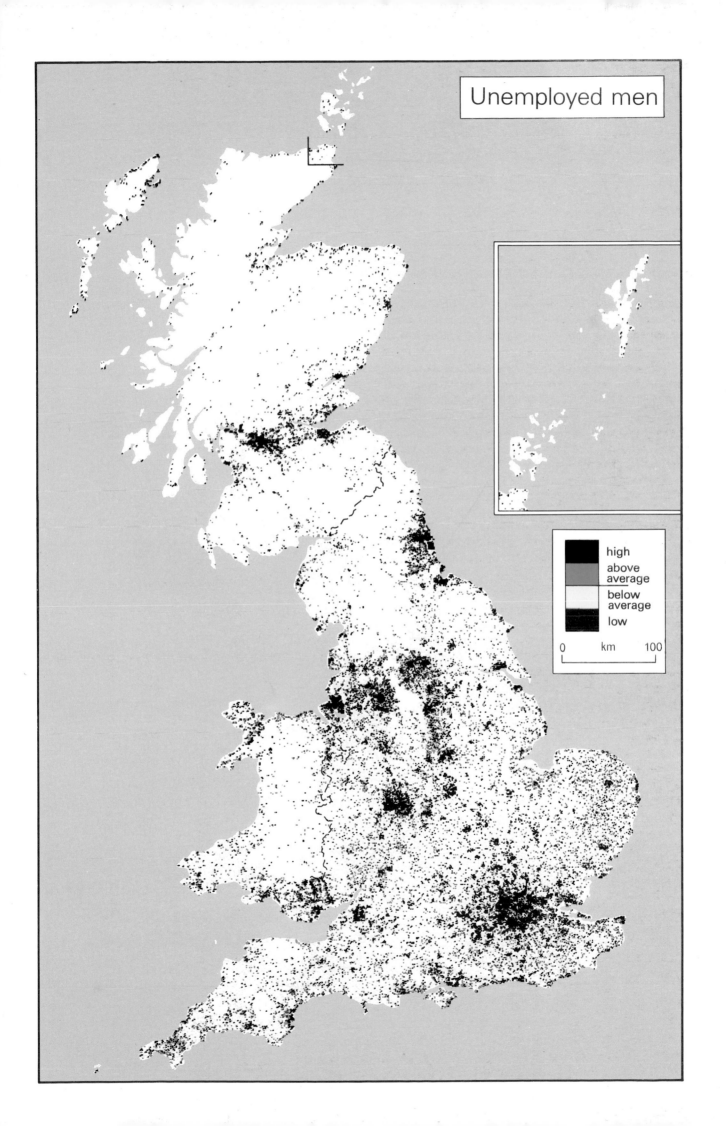

Unemployed men

high
above
average
below
average
low

0   km   100

MAP 22
Car to work

(Signed chi-square)

In addition to a variety of demographic, social, economic and housing data, British censuses have traditionally collected information on the place of work, including, since 1966, data on the mode of transport used between residence and workplace.

This map shows where people lived who travelled to work by car, the most common mode of travel for such journeys. In 1971, in Great Britain as a whole 35.6 per cent of people in employment travelled to work by car. There were considerable variations between parts of the country, the proportion ranging from 29 per cent in Scotland to more than 40 per cent in East Anglia and the South West, and, as the map shows, very pronounced local contrasts. This variety is associated with such inter-related factors as levels of car ownership, the distance travelled, the availability and cost of public transport, and the distribution of places of work and of residence in relation to the road network and other facilities for car users.

In some of the major conurbations, and many smaller towns as well, there is a clear dichotomy between an inner zone of low values and a peripheral suburban belt of high values. London as the largest conurbation is the clearest example, with the most highly developed internal public transport system, a high density of residences and workplaces and with relatively little scope for the use of cars. The same situation is visible, to a varying degree, in such diverse centres as Birmingham, Leicester, Bristol, Plymouth, Southampton, Cardiff and Norwich. In London, small low value areas can be seen within the suburban ring of high car usage; these mark local employment centres and/or nodal points on the metropolitan transport system from which rapid movement to the city centre is possible.

In the northern conurbations, where levels of car ownership are often low, the areas of high car usage are more restricted: in Manchester, people who travel to work by car are concentrated on the southern fringe of the conurbation, on Merseyside in the Wirral peninsula (assisted by the Mersey tunnels) and in Leeds/Bradford in a few more prosperous northern suburbs. In north east England and on Clydeside, low values predominate, reflecting the particularly low levels of car ownership in those regions.

Rural areas do not show many high or low values. In the English lowlands generally, car usage tends to be above average, reflecting the scarcity of public transport, high levels of car ownership and the fact that many who live in rural areas work in nearby towns. In more remote and truly rural districts, where farming is still a leading activity and many people live at or near their workplaces — the Scottish Highlands, the Borders, the Pennines and the interior of Wales — below average levels of car usage are common. Parts of East Anglia and the Weald seem to fall into the same category.

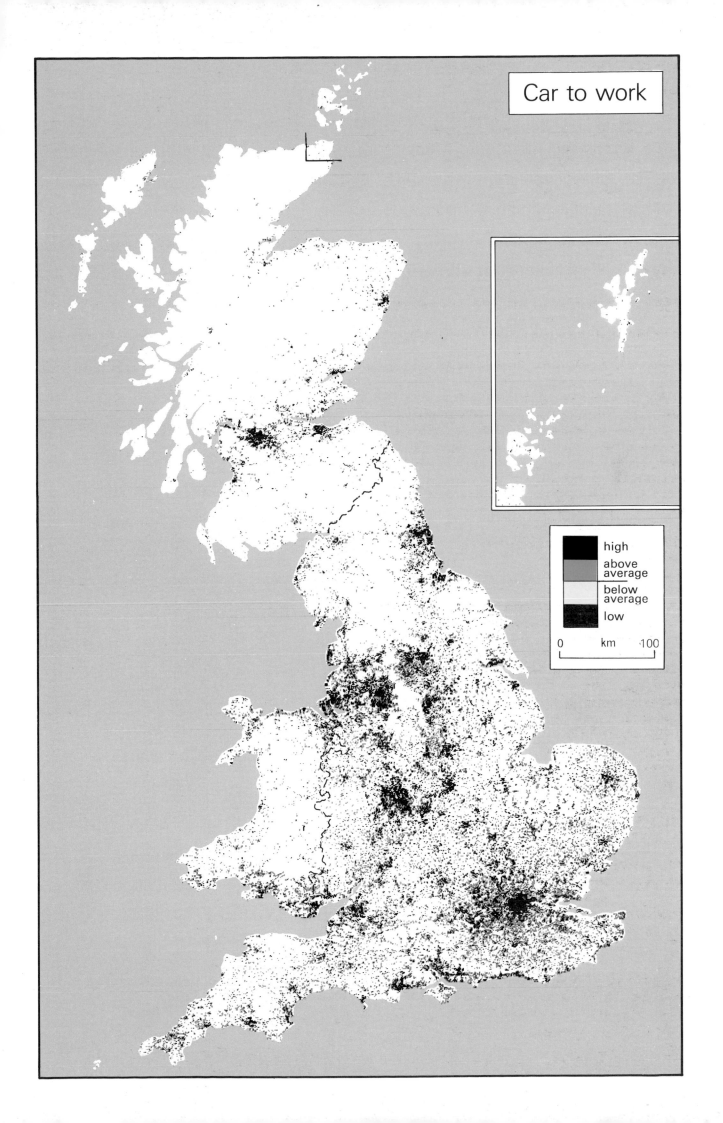

Car to work

high
above
average
below
average
low

0   km   100

MAP 23
Bus to work

(Signed chi-square)

Of the employed population in 1971, 24.7 per cent travelled to work by bus. This map shows where these people lived. Variations were considerably greater than in the case of travel by car: well over 30 per cent used buses in Scotland, Northern England, Yorkshire/Humberside and the North West, but only 19 per cent in the South East and 11 per cent in East Anglia.

The map shows two clear contrasts, which are generally the reverse of Map 22 *Car to Work*. The first is between rural areas and small towns on the one hand, where the level of bus usage is almost universally below average or low, and on the other hand the conurbations, coalfield and industrial areas and large towns which contain practically all the areas of high values. Second, there are marked contrasts within and between the major urban agglomerations. Among the latter, Greater London is unique in showing a predominance of low values, with high values largely confined to the East End.

Areas from which travel by bus is relatively unimportant are visible in the suburban fringes of the West Midlands and the south side of Manchester, but such areas are very largely absent from the York–Notts–Derby coalfield, North West England and the Scottish lowlands, where there are large areas of high values.

It should perhaps be pointed out that the journey to work question in the census seeks information on the mode of travel for the longer part of the individual's journey, so that the rail commuter who has a short bus ride from railway station to office is recorded as travelling to work by train.

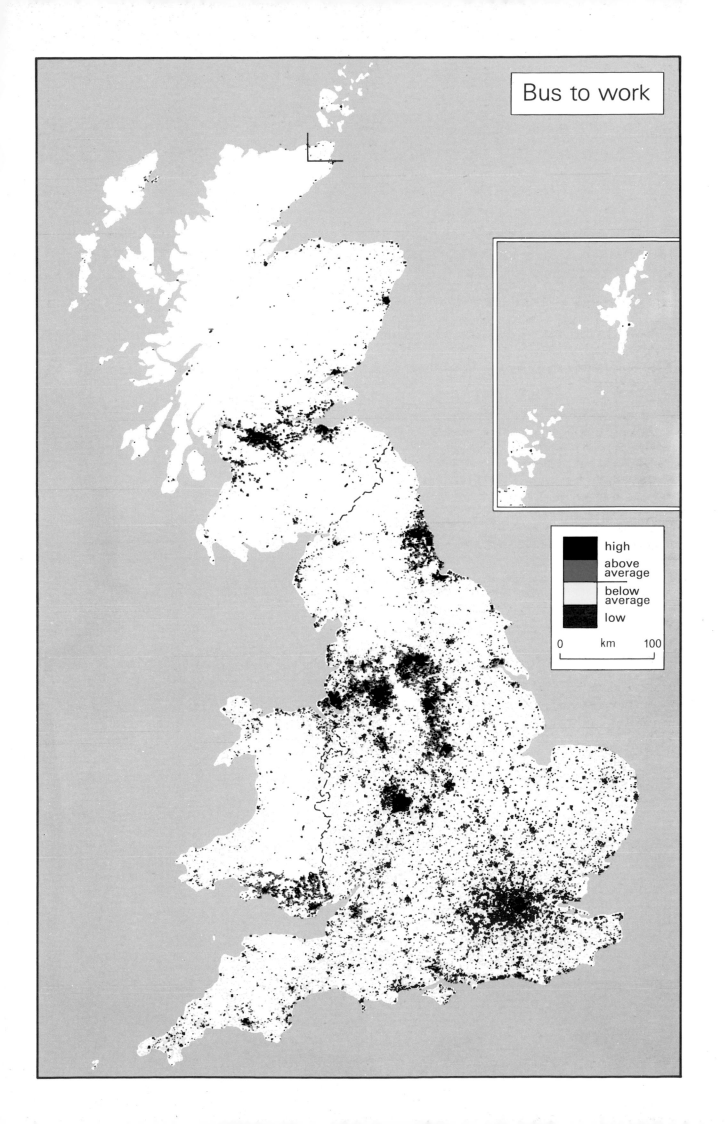

Bus to work

high
above average
below average
low

0   km   100

MAP 24
Train to work

(Signed chi-square)

Of the four travel to work maps, the map showing where people live who travel to work by train is the most striking in the concentration of both high and low values in urban areas, which stand out clearly against a rural background of values near but usually slightly below average. In 1971, only 6.3 per cent of the employed population of Great Britain travelled to work by train, a pronounced decline from the level of earlier censuses, due in part to increased levels of car ownership and also to the wider dispersal of workplaces. The biggest contrast was between the South East, where 15.7 per cent used this mode, and the rest of the country, where the proportion travelling by train varied from 3.4 per cent in Scotland to less than one per cent in Yorkshire/Humberside, in East Anglia, in the East Midlands and in the South West. The proportion using this mode of travel is closely determined by the availability of commuter rail services, which survive only where a very large volume of movement occurs, and the map, in the main, picks out those parts of the country still served by such rail systems. Interestingly, rail use by people living near non-commuter lines can also be identified in some cases. A few squares with above average and high values for travel to work by train are remote from any 1971 passenger service. These squares are likely to represent rail users enumerated away from their usual residences.

By far the largest zone with high values is that centred on London where, beyond a large central core served by the underground system (not distinguished from other types of railway in the census data) strings of high value squares extend outwards in all directions, reaching the Chilterns and beyond, the Essex and Kent coasts of the Thames estuary, and as far as the Channel coast between Worthing, Brighton and Seaford. Elsewhere, commuter rail systems are much less extensive: the best examples are the system to the south of Manchester, the Merseyside system extending from Southport to the Wirral peninsula, and Clydeside downstream of Glasgow to Gourock and Helensburgh. Smaller pockets of high values can be identified in other regions, for example, the Tyneside lines to South Shields, Tynemouth and Whitley Bay and the Saltburn–Redcar areas of Teesside. Less intense, but still above average use of rail transport can also be seen, for example in some of the valleys of South Wales, in the West Midlands, to the east of Nottingham and between Norwich and Great Yarmouth.

In contrast, several major urban agglomerations show low values for travel to work by train, for example, the north east (apart from Lower Tyneside), the York–Notts–Derby coalfield, the Potteries, Leicester, Bristol, Edinburgh and Aberdeen.

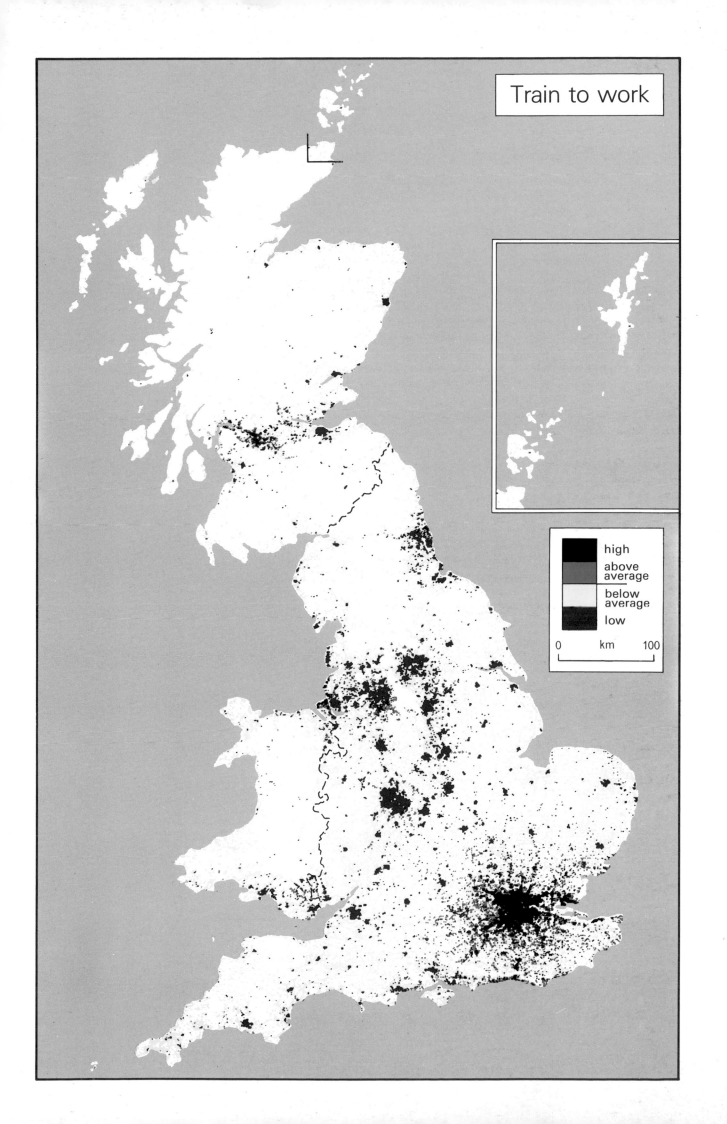

Train to work

high
above average
below average
low

0   km   100

MAP 25

Walking to work

(Signed chi-square)

In 1971, 21 per cent of people in employment walked to work; this map shows where they lived. There were fewer regional variations in this mode of travel than in any other: the lowest proportions were 18.5 per cent in the South East and 19.4 per cent in East Anglia, and the highest 24.6 per cent in Scotland and 23.4 per cent in the north of England. These contrasts are clearly visible on this map, where above average and high values are more common in Scotland and Northern England, while below average and low values are more common in the South East and East Anglia.

The largest area of high values is the Black Country, west of Birmingham. But other industrial areas such as Tyneside, Sunderland, Manchester and Oldham have patches of high values, which are also prominent in central areas of London (especially the East End), Bristol, Birmingham, Liverpool, Hull and Glasgow, in all of which there are striking core-periphery contrasts. In addition, smaller towns throughout Great Britain have high values for people walking to work, as in the widely spread examples of Peterhead, Hawick, Dumfries, Whitby, Bridlington, Sleaford, Bury St Edmunds, Brecon and Yeovil.

Above average values appear as a speckled pattern, but are particularly common on the coalfields. However, the closure of many pits has meant that more miners are going to work by car or bus from what were once pithead settlements so that the coalfields do not stand out as clearly on this map as they might have done when more pits were active. Many of the isolated blue and purple squares in rural areas reflect farming and other populations who work a short distance from their homes. Many more rural areas appear as yellow, reflecting, in part, above average car use indicated in Map 22.

Finally, red squares, indicating low values for walking to work, tend to form continuous areas, as in the suburban rings of London and most other large towns and cities, notably Birmingham, Liverpool, Glasgow, Sheffield and Bristol. Red squares are also quite common in rural commuter areas of England, but not in Scotland.

In summary, the map is an indicator of variations in the separation of homes and workplaces. There is least separation in city cores, small towns and some older industrial areas dating from a time when mass transport was not available, and most separation in the suburbs, themselves a product of mass transport facilities.

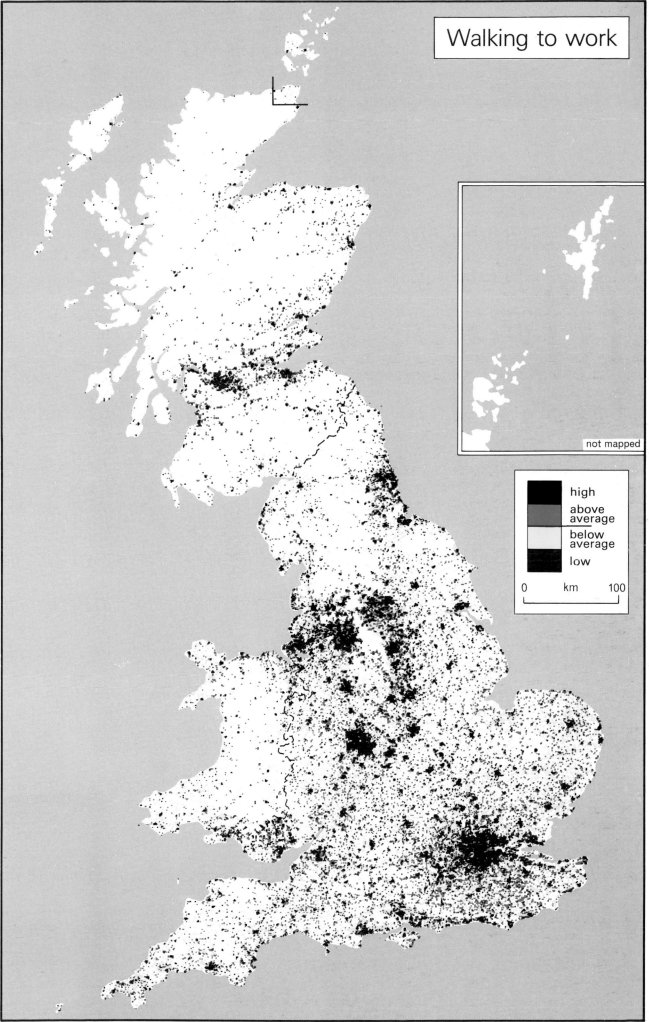

Walking to work

high

above
average

below
average

low

0   km   100

not mapped

MAP 26
Owner—occupiers

(Signed chi-square)

Since the Census counts people at their homes, information on housing conditions is collected during the population census so that the characteristics of housing and population can be related. Households are identified during the census operation as a single person or as a group of people sharing housekeeping, for example, a married couple and their children, or friends sharing a flat. Communal establishments are also identified: hotels, boarding houses, colleges, schools, hospitals, military installations and penal establishments. People living in communal establishments are not included in the information used in the preparation of Maps 26–31.

The 100 per cent SAS give information on the tenure of household accommodation. Of households in Great Britain in 1971, 48 per cent were in owner occupied accommodation, 30 per cent in accommodation rented from a local or public authority, and 21 per cent in accommodation rented, furnished or unfurnished, from a private landlord or company. There is a map showing each of these classes. There are pronounced variations in the pattern of tenure within the major centres of population and between different parts of Britain and there are clear similarities between these patterns and those of other social and economic variables mapped in this atlas.

On the map of owner-occupiers, the most striking contrast is that between Scotland, where only 29 per cent of all households were in owner occupied accommodation, and England and Wales, where the figure was 50 per cent. As a result, areas in Scotland with levels of owner occupation above the average for Britain are very restricted, occurring mainly in western Edinburgh, small sections of suburban Glasgow and in the islands. In England and Wales, on the other hand, high values for owner occupation are widespread, particularly in suburban rings around cities of all sizes and in North Wales, Lancashire, West Yorkshire, the Midlands, Severnside and the south coast. In contrast to such areas, many coalfield districts (South Wales being a notable exception) have low values, as do certain rural areas, especially in the north and Midlands. Low values for owner occupation are also visible in all conurbation cores.

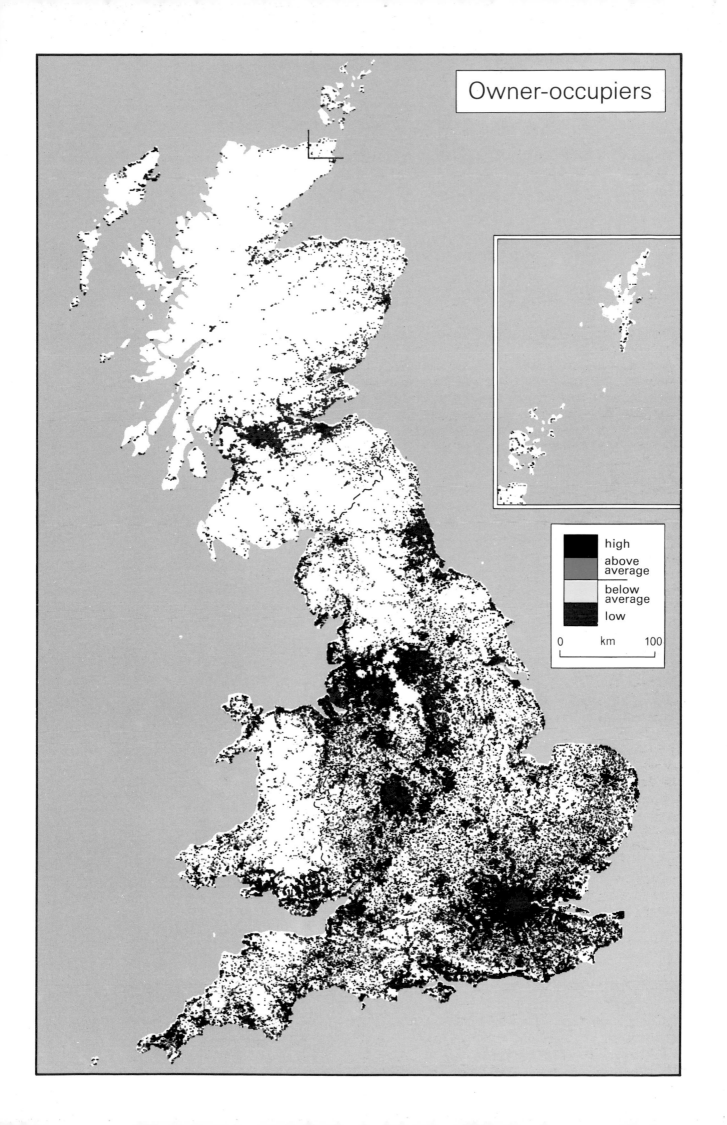

Owner-occupiers

high
above average
below average
low

0   km   100

MAP 27
Council tenants

(Signed chi-square)

This map, showing council tenants, is one of the most strongly polarised maps in the atlas. Most grid squares are in either the high or low category. This is mainly because local authorities have found it convenient to build tracts of council housing, the biggest of which contain many thousands of households, so that this category tends to dominate groups of grid squares. Since nearly 80 per cent of all British households live in owner occupied or council owned accommodation, the map of council tenancy tends to be a mirror image of the owner occupation map (Map 26).

In general terms, council housing tends to be most prominent in densely populated urban areas, particularly where it has replaced slum housing. In Scotland, where 53.4 per cent of all households were council-owned, as against 28.0 per cent in England and Wales, there are relatively few areas where this form of tenancy is not dominant. The extent of high values in the Clydeside conurbation is particularly striking, though there is a strip of low values running north from Thornliebank to Milngavie. In Edinburgh, council housing is concentrated on the east side, and between the two conurbations and on the Fife coalfield the great majority of squares show high values. In rural Scotland there are high values in Caithness and some small towns which contrast with low values in other rural areas such as the Moray Firth, Shetland, Orkney and the Hebrides.

In England, high values for council housing become less frequent towards the south. High values are common in the coalfields and the older industrial areas of the north, particularly the north east, but the largest continuous area of concentrated council housing is in the Black Country. The main concentrations are not generally in conurbation centres but nearby, as around the eastern edge of Liverpool and in east London. South east of Watford, however, such areas are greatly outnumbered by those with low values. The southern and south western coastal strip is particularly prominent in this respect.

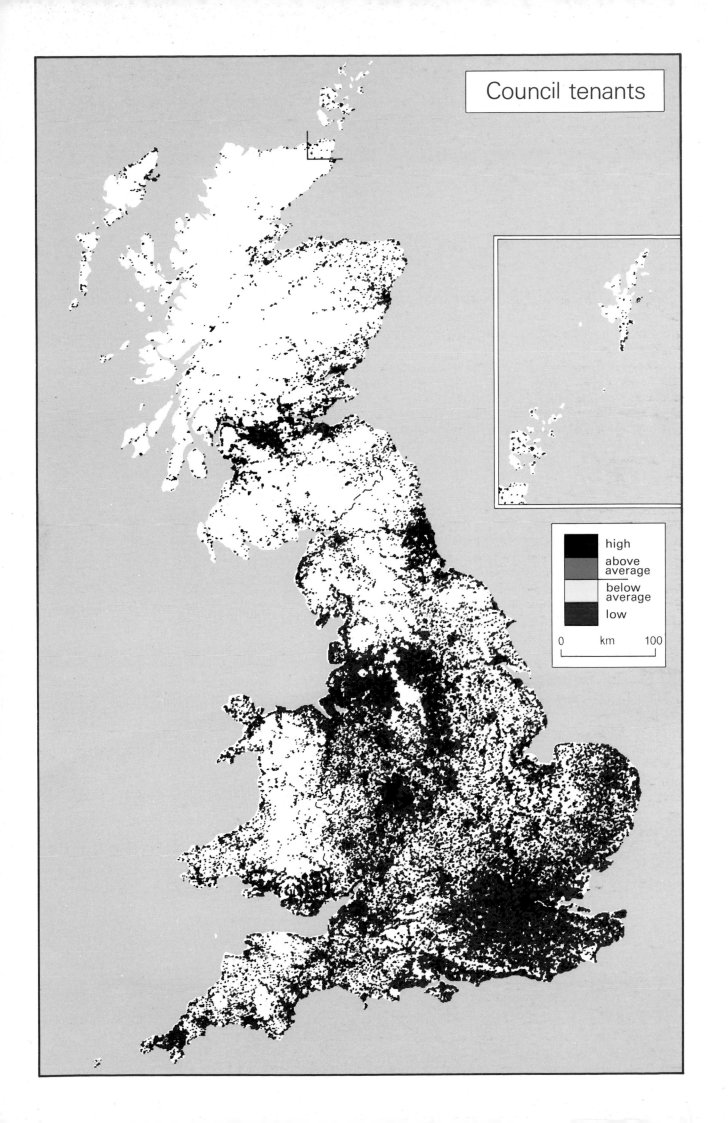

Council tenants

high
above average
below average
low

0   km   100

MAP 28
Private tenants

(Signed chi-square)

This third tenure map shows households renting accommodation from private landlords, whether furnished or unfurnished. Privately rented accommodation is a small and diminishing sector of the British housing stock, mainly as a result of slum clearance and a gradual reduction in the number of small-scale property owners. In 1971, this sector accounted for 21.3 per cent of all households (17.2 per cent in Scotland). A considerably smaller proportion of the total population was living in accommodation rented from private landlords, a relatively large proportion of which was occupied by one-person households.

Renting from private landlords is a feature of the cores of conurbations and cities (down to the size of Grimsby, Lincoln, Bedford and Torbay, for example), but is rare in suburban rings. This pattern is nationwide, and thus provides an excellent indication of the urban structure, showing the dispersed core areas of Yorkshire and Nottinghamshire in contrast to the concentrated cores of Merseyside, Birmingham, Leicester and Hull. But the greatest concentration of private tenants is in Greater London, where an area some 24 km square is dominated by high values. Above average and high values for private tenancy are also very common in many rural areas, as in the Weald, Wiltshire, East Anglia, the Cheshire Plain, the North Pennines and Perthshire.

Local exceptions to the pattern of high values in older urban cores and rural areas include much of South Wales, the Outer Hebrides, and Clydeside outside central Glasgow and Partick.

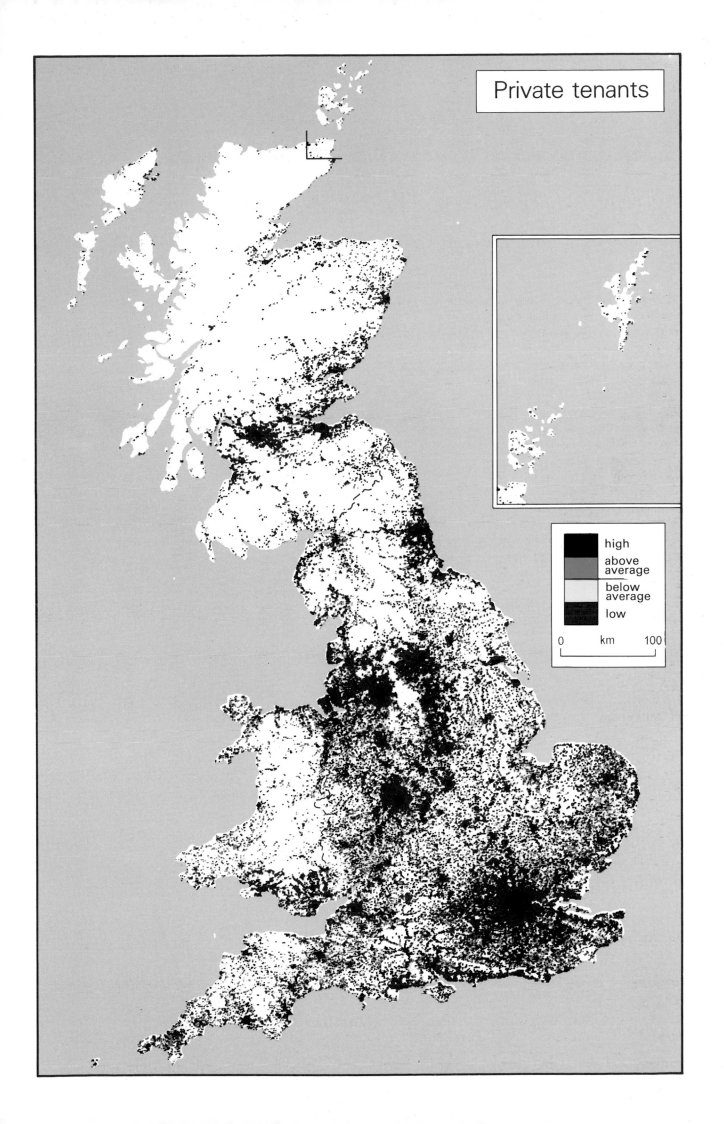

Private tenants

high
above average
below average
low

0   km   100

MAP 29
Household amenities

(Signed chi-square)

This map depicts the pattern of households which have exclusive use of a hot water supply, a fixed bath and an inside WC, such households constituting, in 1971, some 82.5 per cent of the total. This provides an objective, if somewhat crude measure of housing with adequate amenity provision, though there can be wide variations in the standards of the housing included or excluded.

Inner urban areas, where private renting is common, tend to have concentrations of households without the exclusive use of all three amenities, and the contrast with the suburbs is striking. Areas of council housing, on the other hand, usually have all three amenities, even if they exhibit other indications of deprivation, such as overcrowding (Map 31). On the regional scale, amenity provision was low in some of the older industrial areas, such as the South Wales coalfield, Rossendale in Lancashire, west Durham, the Black Country and Cornwall, and low values were also widespread in rural areas of Wales, Cornwall, East Anglia, the Fens, the Peak District, Shetland, Orkney and the Hebrides. Poor housing is thus a rural problem as much as an urban one, though rural south England from Exeter to Essex had mainly above-average values. Low levels of amenity provision sometimes occurred in areas with high levels of owner occupation, as in South Wales and north east Lancashire.

Since 1971, the pattern will have changed as slum clearance and improvements to the housing stock continue, reducing regional and local disparities in amenity provision. But at the same time, in some areas, larger properties have been converted to multiple use, increasing the number of households which share amenities.

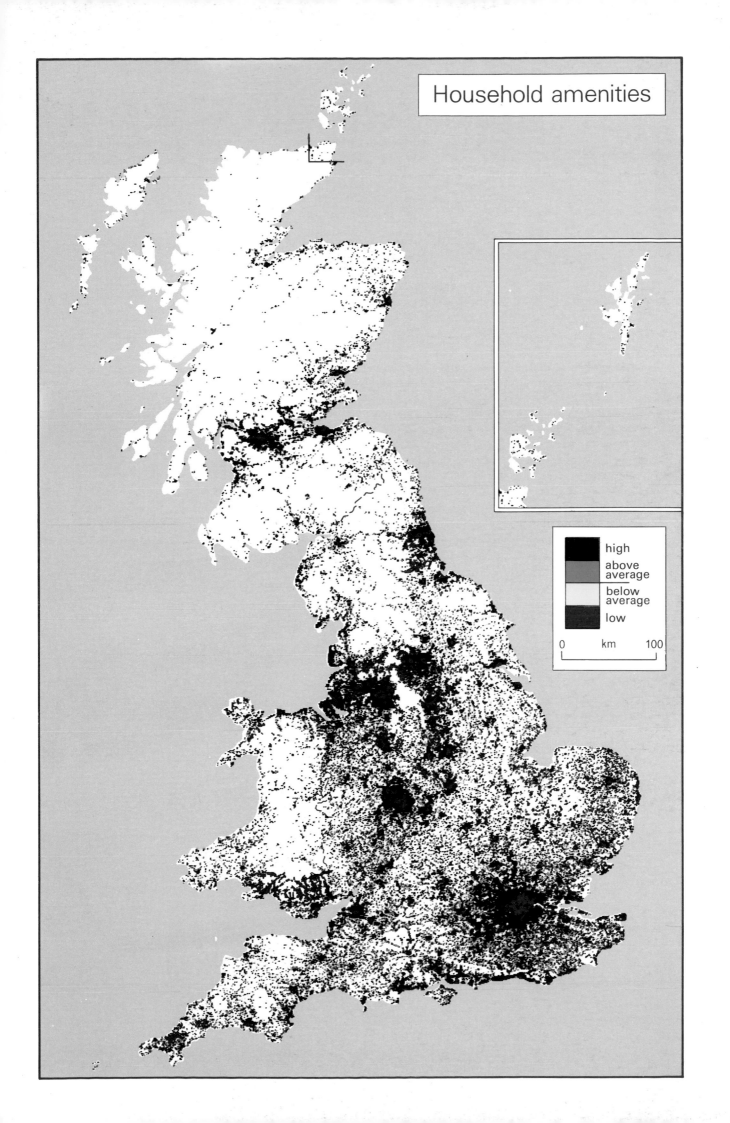

Household amenities

high
above average
below average
low

0   km   100

MAP 30
Households with no car

(Signed chi-square)

Car ownership has been one of the main manifestations of prosperity and changing life styles in post-war Britain. By 1971, when there was one car for every 4.7 people, just over half of all households had a car.

Patterns of car ownership show both regional and local variations. Urban cores and council housing estates have high values for households without cars, and this phenomenon is particularly marked in the coalfields and older industrial areas. North east England, South Lancashire, West Yorkshire and South Wales stand out clearly on the map. In contrast, areas of high owner-occupation, particularly in southern England, have high levels of car ownership — the Home Counties are especially prominent. Rural areas in the main have below average and low values for households without cars, a fact which reflects the lack of rural public transport. Indeed, it has been suggested that public transport in general begins to suffer serious economic difficulties when car ownership passes the level of one car per seven persons. The Hebrides stand out as an exception to the profusion of cars in rural areas, while Cornwall does much better in car ownership than in housing conditions.

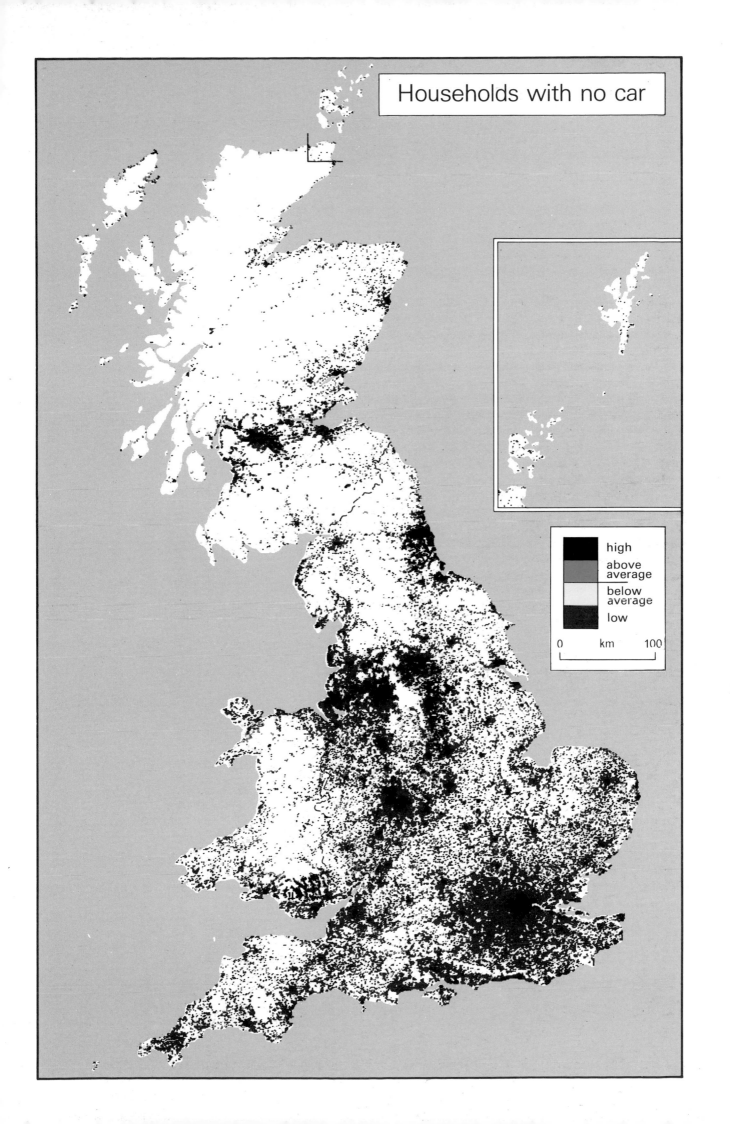

Households with no car

high
above average
below average
low

0   km   100

MAP 31
Overcrowding

(Signed chi-square)

The number of persons per room is a useful indicator of housing standards, and the 1971 Census provided information on the numbers of households living at various levels of density of occupation. This map shows the pattern of households with more than one person per room, which can be regarded as relatively overcrowded, a category constituting 7.2 per cent of all households in Great Britain in 1971. In the 1961 Census, the ratio of 1.5 persons per room was the accepted level of overcrowding, and this change reflects the generally improving standards of housing as well as a decline in the average number of persons per household. Households at this higher level of overcrowding in 1971 were a mere 1.9 per cent of the total.

The map reveals one marked contrast, that between Scotland and the rest of Great Britain. Households with more than one person per room constituted 19.2 per cent of all Scottish households (as against only 6 per cent in England and Wales), as a result of which practically the whole of Scotland has above average or high values for overcrowding on this map. Only suburban areas of west Aberdeen, east Dundee, west Edinburgh, a tiny part of Clydeside and a few smaller towns, for example Perth, have low values for overcrowding by British standards.

In England and Wales, overcrowding is much less extensive. It is most widespread in the north east, which is transitional to Scotland in this respect; elsewhere, high values are characteristic of conurbation cores, where renting from private landlords is common, and of some council housing estates, for example the ring around Liverpool. Throughout rural England and Wales there is a scatter of squares with high values against a background of low values.

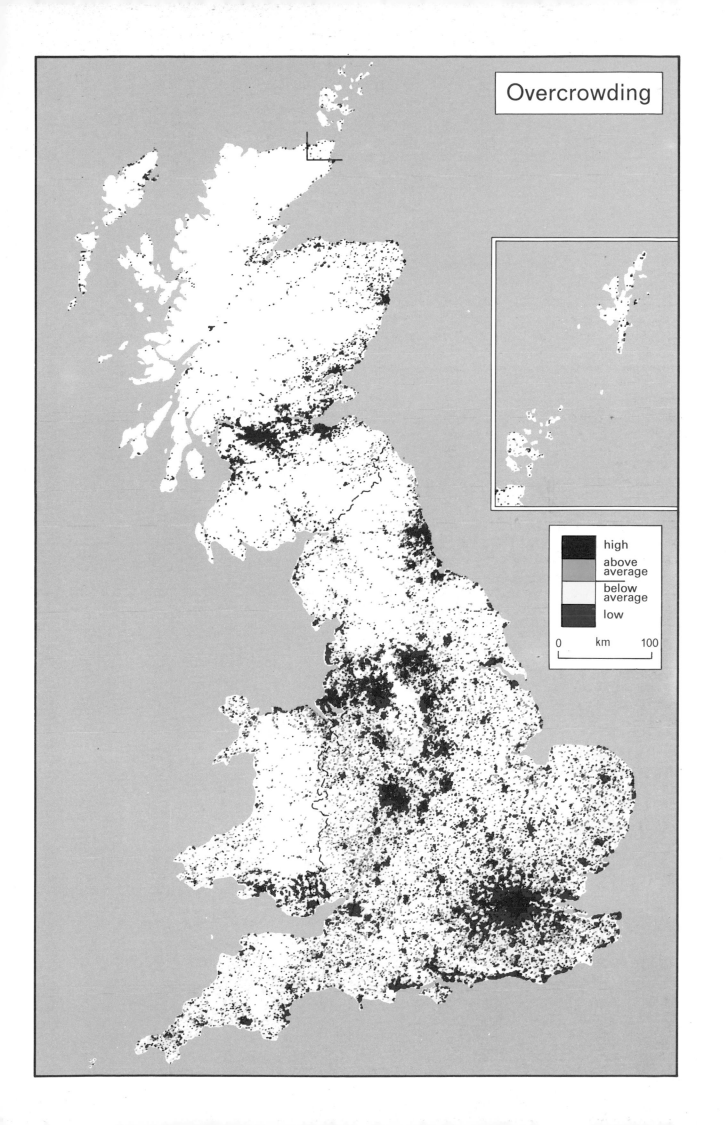

Overcrowding

high
above average
below average
low

0   km   100

MAP 32
Spacious accommodation

(Signed chi-square)

This map is to a large extent a mirror image of Map 31, showing overcrowding, since it portrays the opposite pole of the persons per room indicator, that is households with more than two rooms per person. Such households comprise 34.2 per cent of the total in England and Wales but only 18.7 per cent in Scotland so that high values are virtually absent from Scotland.

However, in many parts of England outside the older urban areas there are numerous squares with near average values of households on both maps 31 and 32, while a few areas, such as central Nottingham and Wallasey, seem to have high values for both overcrowding and spacious accommodation. Most rural areas of England and Wales have above average values for spacious dwellings.

Although it cannot be demonstrated from the Census, these variations seem likely to relate to the age of the accommodation. In areas with a relatively high proportion of newer accommodation, the number of rooms is likely to fit typical modern households; indeed regulations ensure common minimum standards. In areas with more older accommodation there are likely to be greater extremes in the size of units.

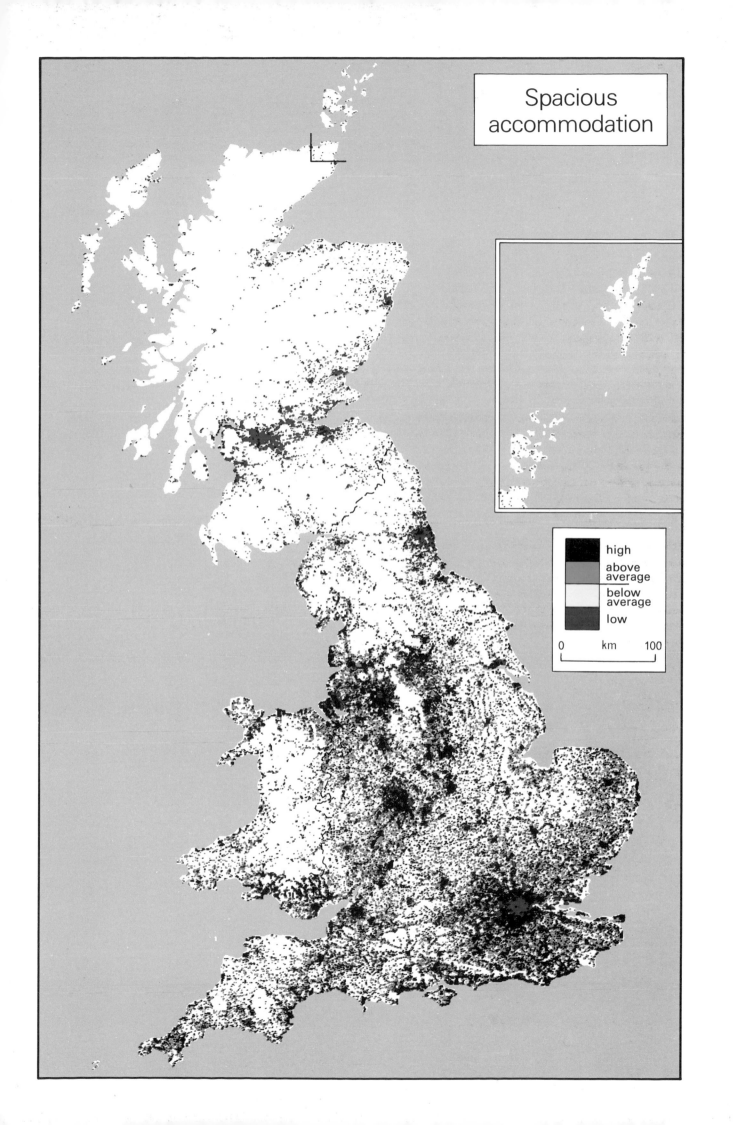

Spacious accommodation

high
above average
below average
low

0   km   100

MAP 33
One-person households

The number of households in Britain has increased rapidly during this century in association with declining family size, reduction in the age of marriage, increasing longevity and the desire of each family unit for a separate home. The number of households more than doubled between 1911 and 1971 and, at the latter date, 17.1 per cent of all households in Britain consisted of only one person, 31.3 per cent of two persons, 19.4 per cent of three, 18.0 per cent of four and 14.2 per cent of five or more members.

One-person households fall into two main types with rather different spatial distributions – which this map combines. There are elderly widowed people, especially women, who are particularly concentrated in retirement areas and areas of high male mortality: this group is significant in accounting for the high values for one-person households along the coasts of southern England, north Wales and west Lancashire (Blackpool and Southport) and, for example, in the towns of east Lancashire and West Yorkshire. There are also the young unmarried individuals, occupants of flats or bedsitters in urban cores, who account for the high values for one-person households in inner London, the central areas of all major cities and many smaller ones.

However, the distribution of one person households in general is associated with the availability of suitable accommodation and there is a fairly close correlation with that of privately rented accommodation. One-person households are generally rare in suburban areas, particularly in new housing estates, and in industrial districts. Values in rural areas are only high where there are retired people.

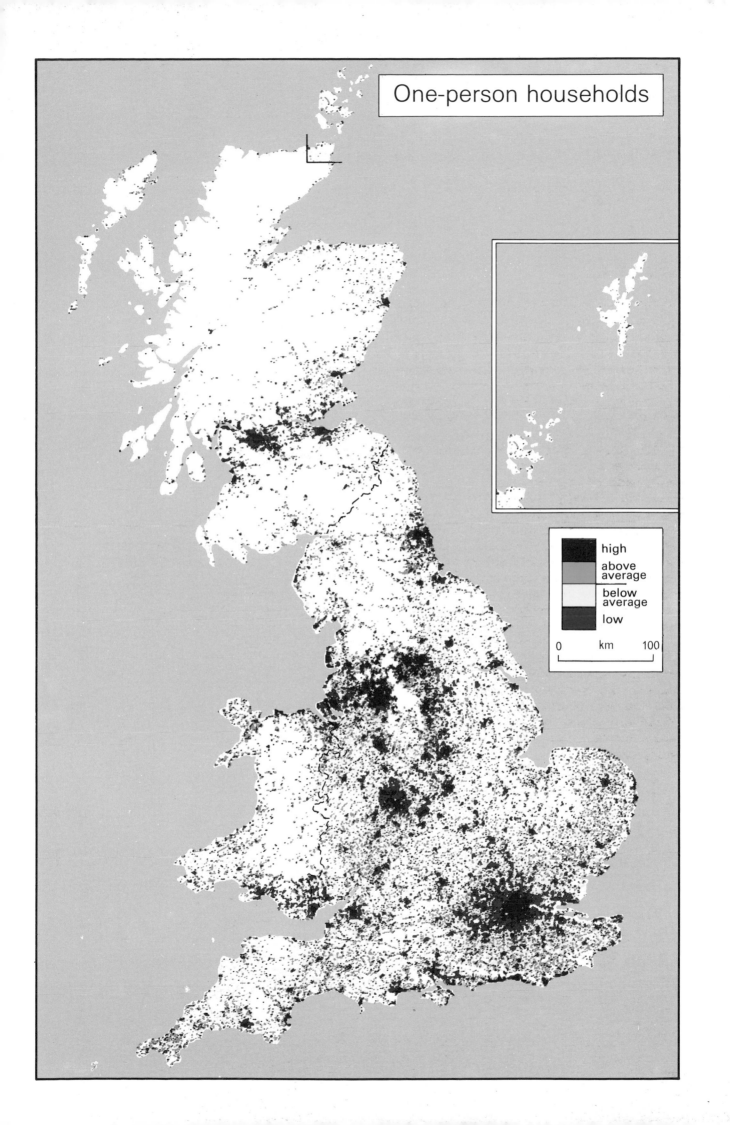

One-person households

high
above average
below average
low

0   km   100

MAP 34
One-parent families

(Absolute numbers: number of one-parent families per kilometre square)

The 1971 Census in Britain counted 627,410 one-parent families with dependent children (children below the age of 15, or above that age if still in fulltime education), representing 8.8 per cent of all families with dependent children. This map shows where this minority group lived.

Of the absolute number maps in this atlas, which, beside depicting total population, are used for showing groups that were not expected to be spread evenly across Britain, the map of one-parent families most resembles the general distribution of population (Map 3). Clusters of one-parent families are found in nearly all urban areas with 50,000 or more people. The clusters are, however, tightly concentrated in the urban cores. The largest area with a continuously high density of one-parent families is inner London. Relatively large high density areas occur in Glasgow, Liverpool, Manchester and Birmingham.

There are few one-parent families in rural areas, especially in Wales, northern England and Scotland; few in coastal areas with concentrations of the elderly, and, it seems, few in some coalfield areas such as the Welsh valleys, Nottinghamshire, Derbyshire and South Yorkshire.

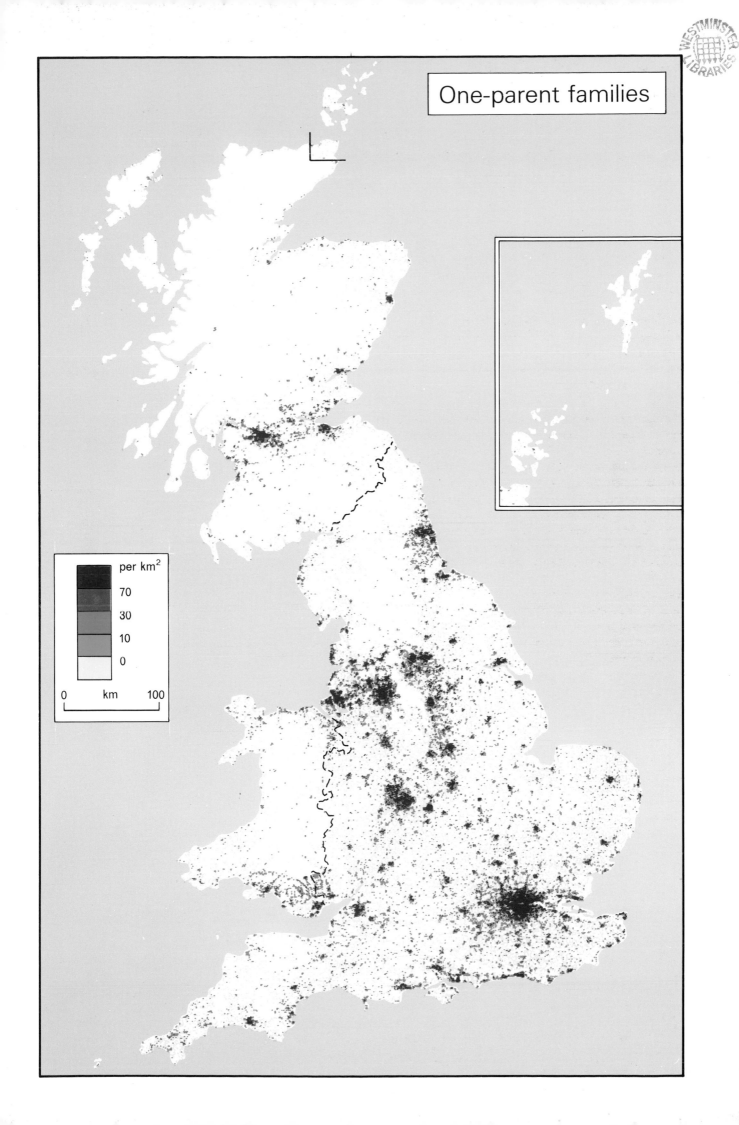

One-parent families

per km²

70

30

10

0

0   km   100

PART 2

Regional maps

Introduction   *page* 87

1 Central South Coast
Population density   92
Born outside the UK   92
Multi-car households   93
Bath-deficient households   93

2 London
Population density   96
Born outside the UK   96
Multi-car households   97
Bath-deficient households   97

3 South Wales – Severnside
Population density   100
Born outside the UK   100
Multi-car households   101
Bath-deficient households   101

4 English Midlands
Population density   104
Born outside the UK   104
Multi-car households   105
Bath-deficient households   105

5 Lancashire – Yorkshire
Population density   108
Born outside the UK   108
Multi-car households   109
Bath-deficient households   109

6 Northern England
Population density   114
Born outside the UK   114
Multi-car households   115
Bath-deficient households   115

7 Central Scotland
Population density   118
Born outside the UK   118
Multi-car households   119
Bath-deficient households   119

Introduction

To complement the national patterns shown on the maps of Great Britain and enlarge on the immense amount of detail within these patterns, a series of maps at four-fold enlargement (a scale of 1:984,000, or approximately 1:1 million) forms the second part of the atlas. The maps were created by the methods described on pages 5 to 8. On these maps, individual squares are clearly identifiable, not so large as to be obtrusive and unnatural, but large enough to be counted. Boundaries for post-1974 counties (post-1975 regions in Scotland) and certain rivers and key roads are included on these regional maps, and the pattern of squares can be related to them.

There are seven sets of regional maps, each region covering an area 173 km × 116 km, as shown on the key map (overleaf). These areas incorporate all the major conurbations and include 87 per cent of the population of Great Britain (46.8 million of a total of 54.0 million). The maps have been positioned so as to maximise the number of unsuppressed grid squares in each, and to show urban regions undivided wherever possible. For each area there is a key place-name map indicating the main towns.

On all regional maps the position of national grid lines is indicated in the margins. For each area there are four standard maps on two facing pages. Each is a section of a national map. In assigning a colour to each square the value for that square is compared with the values in all squares in Great Britain for which data are available. Thus, where there is marked contrast between regions, a map may show few squares above (or below) the national average.

The first map, *Population density,* uses a different set of classes from the national map (Map 3). The other three maps show variables not mapped at the national level, but which are particularly relevant to the main centres of population and show clear patterns in these areas. These three are all chi-squared maps.

The map *Born outside the United Kingdom* includes all those born abroad, regardless of nationality or ethnic origin, who were enumerated in each region at the time of the 1971 Census. In addition to the contrasts within each region, which are discussed on the appropriate page, there are marked differences between the regions, notably the generally low values for those born abroad and living in Northern England or Central Scotland as against the widespread high values found in London and the Midlands.

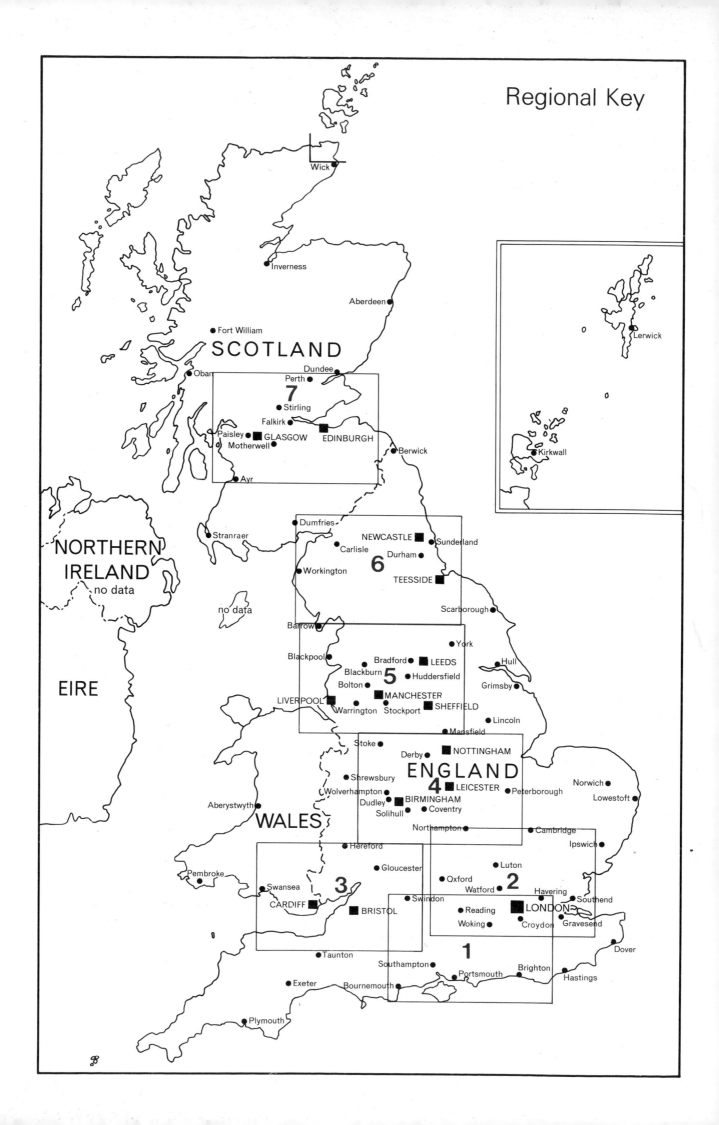

Regional Key

The map *Multi-car households* shows the distribution of house-holds with access to two or more cars, and thus tends to indicate the most prosperous areas. There is a close, though not perfect, negative correlation with the national map *Households with no car* (Map 30).

Finally, the map *Bath-deficient households* provides a powerful indication of poor housing; households which share a bath are included, as well as those which lack one. There has been a decline in the number of bath-deficient households, evident from comparing the 1971 figures with those from earlier censuses. The improvement or clearance of poor housing continued after 1971 but regional differences tend to persist and the census informa-tion remains a significant illustration of relative patterns.

Region: area covered	Population	Number of populated squares
1 Central South Coast 395 to 568 km E 075 to 191 km N	12,381,972	14,159
2 London 439 to 612 km E 147 to 263 km N	14,036,453	16,828
3 South Wales–Severnside 257 to 430 km E 130 to 246 km N	4,040,409	13,755
4 English Midlands 362 to 535 km E 245 to 361 km N	8,008,416	16,954
5 Lancashire–Yorkshire 299 to 472 km E 360 to 476 km N	11,073,677	14,060
6 Northern England 296 to 469 km E 475 to 591 km N	3,167,813	11,034
7 Central Scotland 208 to 381 km E 619 to 735 km N	4,167,957	9,757

Keys to the Regional Maps

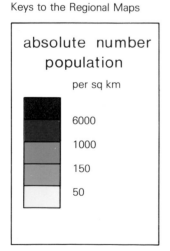

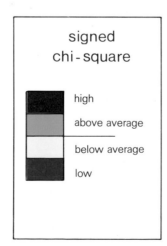

Overlaps between regions

Regions 1 and 2	9,092,117	5,286
Regions 1 and 3	315,417	1,336
Regions 2 and 4	562,963	2,546
Regions 3 and 4	12,501	58
Regions 4 and 5	48,990	97
Regions 5 and 6	4,591	81
Total mapped	**46,840,118**	**87,143**
Percentage of GB	**86.8**	**57.2**

REGION 1
Central South Coast

The maps of the Central South Coast region depicted here include much of London and thus this is the second most popular regional area of the seven portrayed in this atlas. Its 13,985 populated squares contained 12.4 million people (23 per cent of the GB total) in 1971 at an average density of 888 per populated sq km, the highest of the seven regional areas portrayed in this atlas. However, nine million of these lived in the area also covered by the maps of London and are referred to mainly on pages 94 and 95. A further 315,000 lived in the area which is also portrayed in the maps of South Wales–Severnside.

Population density

The most striking feature of the population density map is the line of coastal towns broken only by the New Forest in the west and by Beachy Head and the South Downs in the south east. In the south west the Poole-Bournemouth-Christchurch agglomeration,

all now part of Dorset, stretches for more than 20 km from east to west, and 10 km or more inland to the edges of the New Forest. To the north east of the Solent, in South Hampshire, is an area of high densities, almost on the scale of a conurbation, from Totton and Eastleigh through Southampton, Fareham, Gosport and Portsmouth to Havant and Emsworth, with Winchester an outlier. In West Sussex, the line of towns is less continuous, and densities are mixed – Chichester, Bognor Regis and Littlehampton can all be distinguished. However, from Worthing eastwards, Brighton and Hove dominate the coastal strip to the point where the south Downs meet the coast, beyond which Eastbourne is the major centre. In all this line of coastal towns, the only extensive areas of very high density (over 6000 per sq km) are in Brighton and Southampton, and especially in Portsmouth.

Outside Greater London, the other main area of higher densities is that of Reading–Wokingham–Camberley–Farnborough–Aldershot. Elsewhere, the larger patches of red (1001–6000 per sq km) indicate the pattern of towns of importance at county or local level, like Swindon, Newbury, Andover, Salisbury, Basingstoke, Guildford, Reigate, Crawley and Tonbridge. The influence of London is also seen in the blue and green (26–1000 per sq km) aureole around the capital, where there are few uninhabited patches – even the line of the North Downs is not clearly visible – and such densities are very much more common there than elsewhere on the map, except in the South Hampshire Basin and near the major coastal towns. In the western part of the map, the influence of relief on density is very clear. Large areas of downland – Cranborne Chase, Salisbury Plain, Marlborough Downs, Berkshire Downs, Hampshire Downs and South Downs (stretching eastward right across the map) – show as extensive uninhabited or thinly settled areas, separated by lines of settlement along valleys, such as the Vale of Pewsey and the valleys of the Thames, Avon and Test and their tributaries. At the small scale, the Isle of Wight's intricate pattern of population density epitomises this marked influence of relief.

Born outside the United Kingdom

The map of persons born outside the United Kingdom is dominated by the large concentration of purple squares, indicating high values in central and west London. High values also occur in many towns to the west and south west of London, such as Reading, Camberley, Farnborough, Aldershot and Guildford and in areas between. This spread of the cosmopolitan character of London into what are generally high status areas may partly reflect the residences of overseas born employees of the many international and foreign companies located in and to the west of London.

Further west, high values stand out in Swindon and the military centres of Salisbury Plain, notably Tidworth, mainly because of the presence of children born overseas to British service families and because of the presence of overseas born wives of service men. Along the south coast, people born abroad are particularly concentrated in the centres of the two major seaside resorts, Brighton and Bournemouth, and of the smaller resorts of Eastbourne and Worthing, where it is likely that there are concentrations of foreign born students and workers in service industries. These resorts are also, to some extent, outposts of cosmopolitan London. However, other parts of the coastal belt have low values of people born abroad. The other main concentrations of purple squares are in central Southampton and Portsmouth and in some of the smaller settlements in the New Forest, such as Lymington, where there are probably a number of retired people born abroad.

Multi-car households

There can be little doubt that the Central South Coast region contains many households with the means to have two or more cars and this is reflected in the map of multi-car households, where high values are dominant. The wide commuter belt to the south and west of London is particularly striking in this respect, and the purple and blue patches stretch right out to the South Downs in the south and to Newbury in the west. High values are also common in the suburban outskirts of the south coast towns, and quite common in many of the remaining rural areas. In contrast, there are, apart from London, few areas with low values, save in the central areas of the major south coast towns, like Bournemouth, Southampton, Portsmouth, Worthing, Brighton and Eastbourne, and in the central parts of the main inland towns, like Swindon, Reading, Basingstoke and Aldershot. In addition, some of the military centres of Salisbury Plain have low values.

Bath-deficient households

The pattern of values on the map of households which share or lack a fixed bath is largely the antithesis of that of multi-car households, and below average and low values are preponderant. Only the map of Central Scotland has a larger proportion of unsuppressed squares with below average values. The purple squares indicate that, in 1971, high values for bath-deficient households were found mainly in the most densely peopled central areas of the main towns and cities, including seaside resorts like Bournemouth, Brighton and Eastbourne. The vivid contrasts in the concentric pattern around London – solid purple central areas, red in its suburban ring, and the outermost belt of largely yellow and red – is mirrored to a lesser extent in most of the other towns. There is a sprinkling of purple squares over many of the rural areas, revealing that there were still pockets of poorer housing, especially along the eastern fringe of the map, in East Sussex and West Kent.

Population density

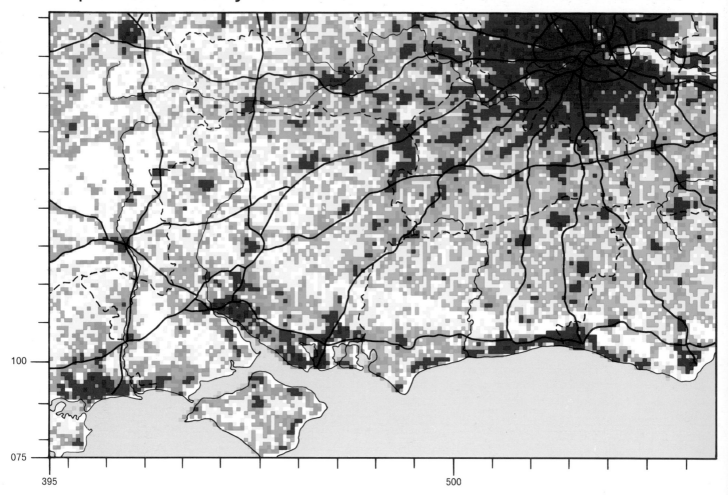

Born outside the U.K.

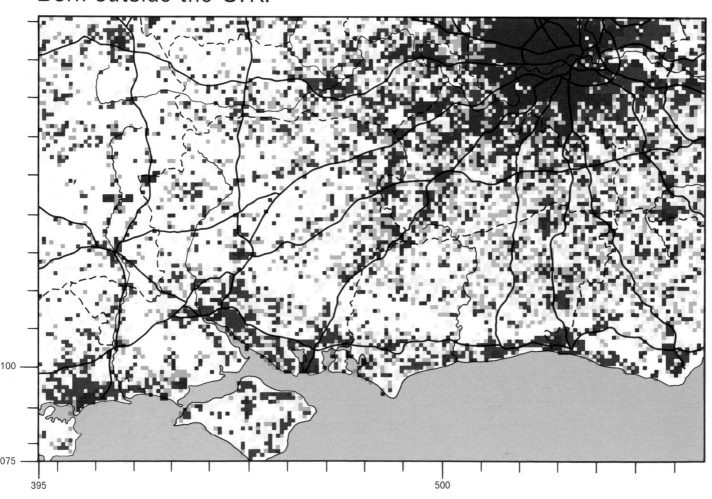

Multi-car households

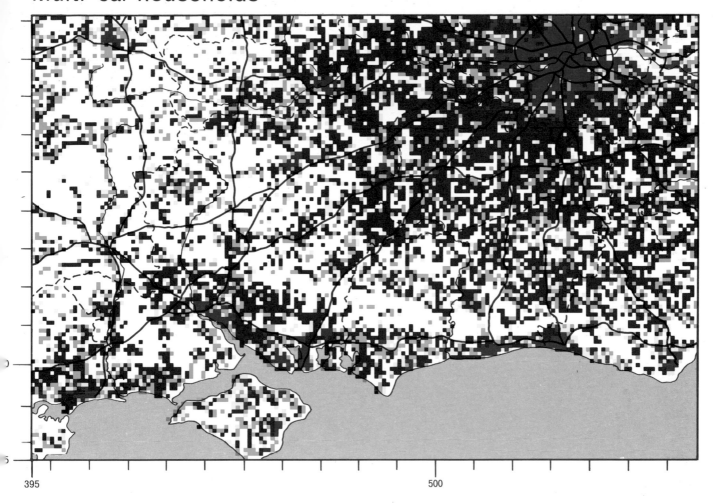

395   500

Bath deficiency

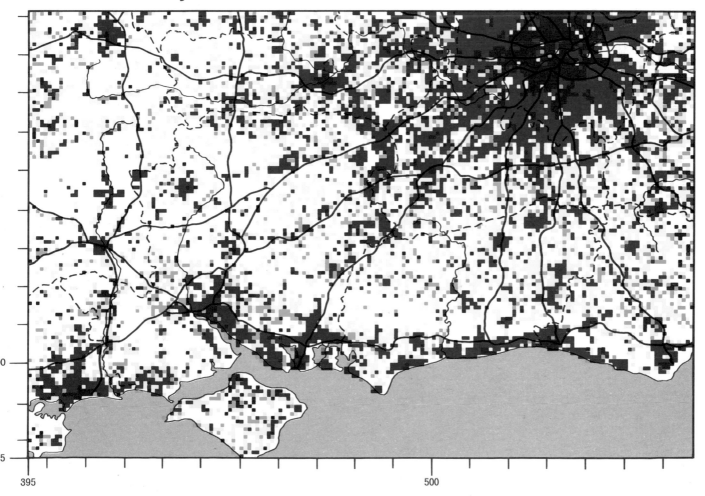

395   500

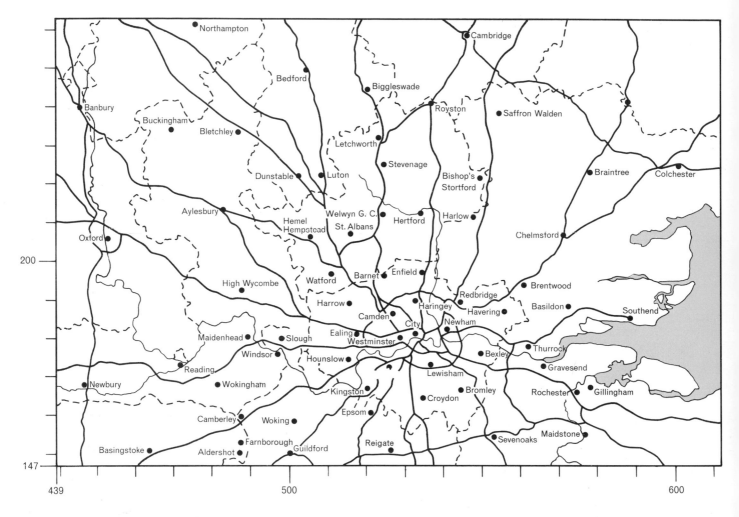

The area covered by the regional map of London and the northern Home Counties has the largest population of the seven regional areas mapped. It contained 14 million people in 1971 – a quarter of the population of Britain – at an average density of 842 people per sq km in the 16,632 populated squares.

The maps are dominated by the mass of London and by the concentric and radial patterns around it. Such dominance is not found in other regional maps, although the influence of London extends over a considerable part of the Central South Coast mapped on pages 90 to 93, and the maps of the two areas have to be taken together to see the regional focus on London.

Population densities

The map shows a general gradation from the high densities of inner London to the lower densities of the outer Home Counties. This is modified by irregular radiating zones of high densities, with interstices of lower densities, reaching through London's satellites towards the regional centres of the South East.

All but a handful of the 544 one kilometre squares (black) on the map with over 6000 people are within Greater London, and most are concentrated in a 10 kilometre wide belt of continuous high density which almost circles the small, lower density commercial core of the cities of London and Westminster. The belt is elongated eastward and westward into easier, and early developed, terrain. The Thames and the Lea mark the major breaks in the belt, with non-residential riverside land uses such as docks, warehouses, factories, waterworks, parks and recreation grounds. Low hills with their areas of open land and lower-density development are visible on the margins of the belt.

Within the high density belt are areas with well over 10,000 people per sq km, characterised by large nineteenth century houses subdivided into flats or bedsitters, and by purpose built flats. But areas characterised by unbroken two storey terraced housing built before 1914, such as Newham, also come within the belt.

Outside the high density belt, and covering most of the remaining areas of Greater London, is a ring dominated by densities between 1001 and 6000 people per sq km (red), characteristically developed between 1919 and 1939 with more generous use of land than previously. But the frequency of areas with densities above 6000 people per sq km indicates the variability of densities in outer London. Some high densities mark older centres, such as Kingston and Enfield, engulfed by the outward spread of London; others indicate the 'random' intersection of the mixture of residential and non-residential land uses with the grid squares, augmented by high rise building — the sector around Harrow typifies such patterns. The major open spaces of various types in outer London can be seen: from the unpopulated banks of the Thames estuary clockwise through the outer parts of Bromley, including Biggin Hill; Mitcham Common; Richmond and Bushey parks; Heathrow airport; the Harefield area; the Totteridge area; Enfield Chase; and Epping Forest.

The radial zones of higher densities combine long established service and industrial centres, suburbs associated with commuter rail services, new towns of various vintages, and the infill of newer owner occupied housing. Prominent in the east is the zone of commuter towns towards Southend on the north side of the Thames estuary, and the more industrial zone towards Gillingham on the south side of the Thames estuary. Prominent in the north is a zone along the A1, including four new towns, towards Letchworth, and a broad zone towards Luton. Prominent in the west is a zone through industrial Slough towards Reading; and in the south a zone through Woking towards Aldershot.

Unpopulated areas (white) and areas with less than 25 people per sq km (yellow) have little form. Relief, obvious in other regional maps, hardly intrudes. There are larger areas with densities less than 25 people per sq km to the north and north east of London than elsewhere around it, and the sector of Essex extending outward from Redbridge between Harlow and Chelmsford, is the least densely populated area near to London.

Around London there is a greater spread of intermediate densities between 26 and 1000 people per sq km (blue/green) than in any other region mapped. Such densities are particularly characteristic of the whole area south of the Thames, spreading well into the Weald, and of the Chilterns. There is no general arrangement between the blue and green squares — indicating the 'random'

effect of grid squares intersecting with a settlement and density pattern varying over short distances.

As well as an expression of proximity to London and other centres, it is possible to see the underlying divide on the map between dominantly blue/green areas and dominantly yellow/-white areas. The former broadly reflect the poor and indifferent agricultural land — for example, in the Chilterns, east Berkshire, Surrey and the Weald — where development in the last two centuries has spread widely in the heathlands and low hills; at first these areas offered unfettered opportunities for settlement and then came to be regarded as desirable residential locations. The yellow/white areas reflect the better land and the associated tendency for earlier settlements to be in the form of villages.

In all, the population density map of the London region offers an opportunity for the actual imprint of development to be compared with the policy intentions for bounding London with a Green Belt and encouraging the growth of new towns in relative isolation from London.

Born outside the United Kingdom
The map of those born outside the UK is dominated by the zone, at least 30 kilometres across in all directions, of continuous high values marking the cosmopolitan centre and west of London, and reflecting its role as an international centre. High values spread to the west and south west of London — the map of the Central South Coast on page 92 shows the full extent of this spread. In marked contrast, low values predominate in east London, in parts of south and south east London, and to the east of London. High values mark the university towns of Oxford and Cambridge, industrial centres like Bedford and Luton and places in which the armed forces are present such as Chatham and north east Oxfordshire. In all, some 38 per cent of the unsuppressed one kilometre squares have above average or high values, a somewhat lower proportion than the Central South Coast regional map which contains most of Greater London and the area to the south west.

The concentration in Greater London of people born in the Commonwealth, in the Irish Republic, in Europe and elsewhere in the world was clear from the published statistics of the 1971 Census. The map illustrates this, but it shows the east-west difference outside London which is less easy to discern in the published statistics. This east-west contrast may lie in differences in prosperity, employment opportunities and status of areas in the years before the 1971 Census: for example jobs were available for immigrants in the growth areas to the west of London; and many international and foreign firms are located in and to the west of

Population density

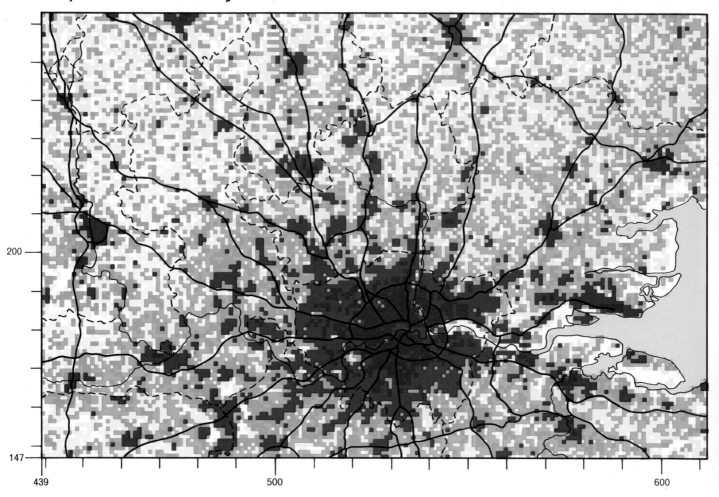

Born outside the U. K.

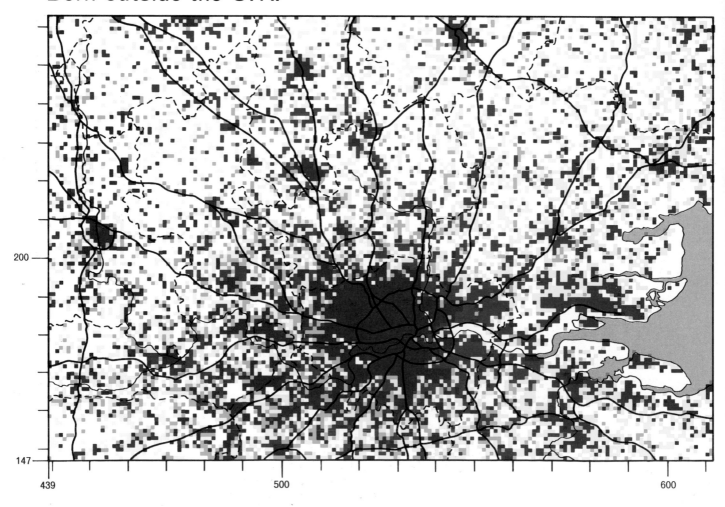

Multi-car households

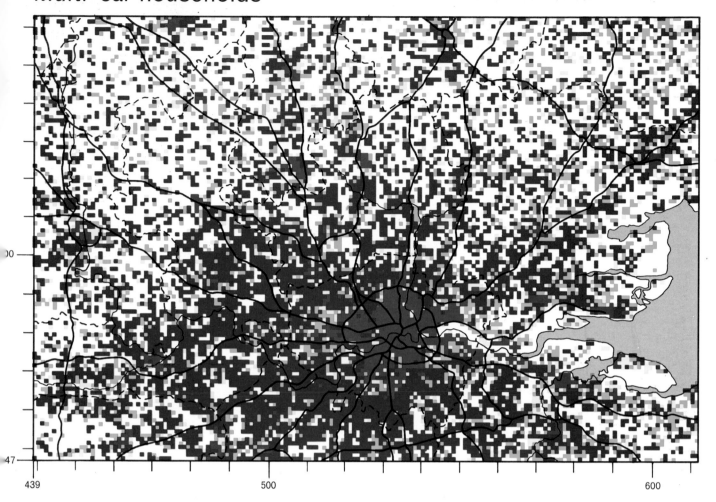

Bath deficiency

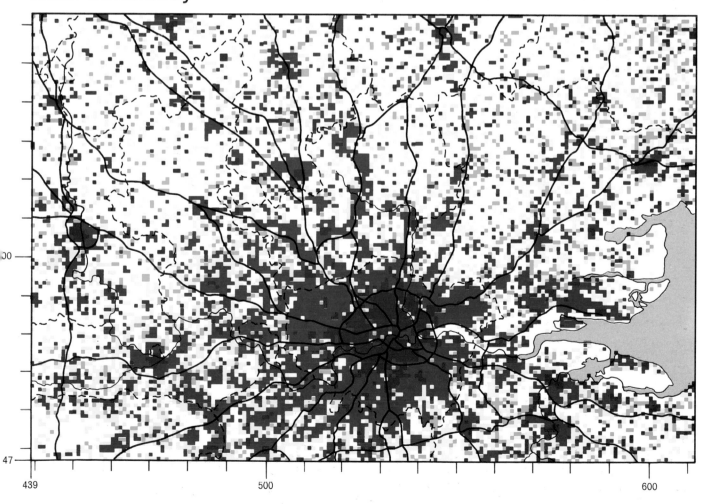

London and their overseas born employees may live in the higher status residential areas.

Multi-car households

The pattern is clear cut; the inner, densely populated areas of London and other towns of the region are marked by low values; almost the whole of the rest of the region has above average values, with a notable expanse of high values to the west and south west of London.

High values for multi-car households indicate a prosperous population in which there are relatively few people of pensionable age and relatively few one- and two-person households. They also indicate a need for personal transport in the loose urban structure where jobs, shops and schools are some distance from homes, typical of much of the Home Counties. The low values of central London cannot be interpreted as indicating only a lack of prosperity — few of west London's high status areas show up — but relate to the relative frequency of one- and two-person households and households of people of pensionable age, and to the lack of facilities for the use of cars together with the relative abundance of public transport.

The relative frequency of below average and low values along the south side of the Thames estuary and the Medway valley, is perhaps indicative of some difference between the socio-economic character of that area and other parts of the London region.

Bath-deficient households

This map reflects the age and standard of households' accommodation and the distribution of bedsitter-type accommodation where bathrooms are shared between households. Thus inner London with much older housing and shared accommodation, together with extensions in such areas as Ealing, Richmond and Kingston, stands distinct as an area of high values from its newer suburban ring which is dominated by low values. The high status area of inner west London and the widely re-built dockland are, however, distinct as low value areas.

Central parts of many other towns in the region are marked by high values, particularly Reading, Oxford, Luton, Bedford, Cambridge, Southend and the Medway towns, each in turn surrounded by low values. The mixture of values in the less urban parts of the Home Counties, with a considerable number of very high value squares in mid-Bedfordshire and in parts of Cambridgeshire, Essex, Suffolk and north Kent, indicates a lack of amenities in unconverted older rural housing.

South Wales–Severnside

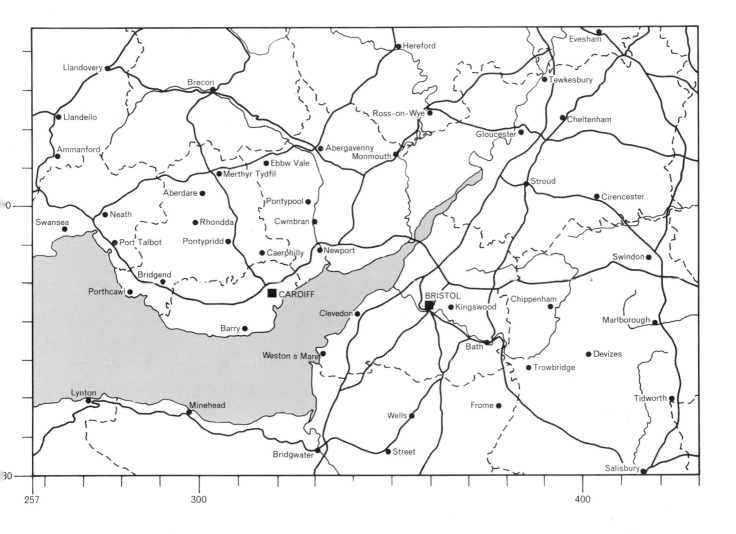

This region is bisected by the estuary of the River Severn and includes most of the populous areas of South Wales along with Avon and most of the English counties of Hereford and Worcester, Gloucester, Wiltshire and Somerset. The whole area contained some 4 million people in 1971 in 13,435 populated one kilometre squares at the comparatively low average density of 298 per populated sq km. About 300,000 people in the south east corner of this region, in Wiltshire, also appear in the map of the Central South Coast region.

Population density
Perhaps the two features most impressively reflected in the map of population distribution and density in this region are relief and mining, although the two regional capitals, Cardiff and Bristol, are also very prominent. In South Wales there are a number of coastal ports and industrial centres which stand out as large patches of red (1001–6000 persons per sq km) around small nuclei of black (over 6000 per sq km): Swansea, Port Talbot, Barry, Cardiff and Newport. Very striking are the lines of red and green which indicate the high densities of the towns lining the Welsh mining valleys, the largest of which are Merthyr Tydfil, Rhondda, Ebbw Vale and Pontypridd, and the uninhabited (white) or thinly peopled (yellow) interfluves. The lines of red and green one kilometre squares do not reflect the linearity of the narrow valleys exactly, but valley orientation is nevertheless very clear. North of the coalfield lie the large uninhabited areas of the Black Mountains and Brecon Beacons, separated by the low rural densities of valley populations, among which only Llandeilo, Llandovery and Brecon stand out as red squares. East of the coalfield, a densely peopled zone lies north of Newport in Gwent, linking with Pontypool and the New Town of Cwmbran and forming an eastern limit to the main areas of high densities.

Population density

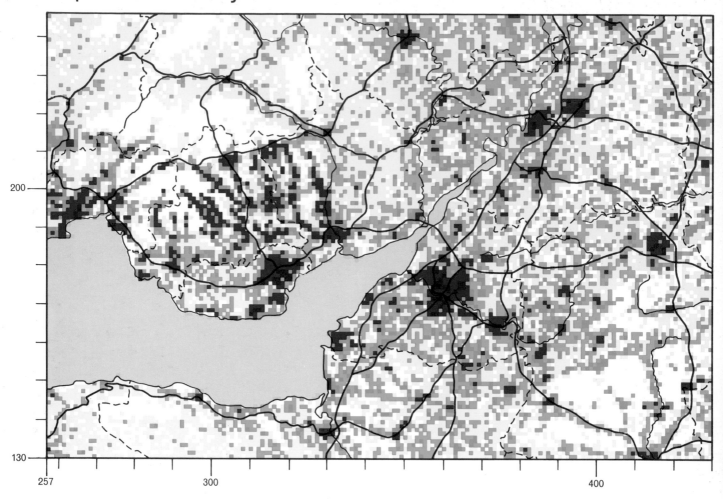

Born outside the U.K.

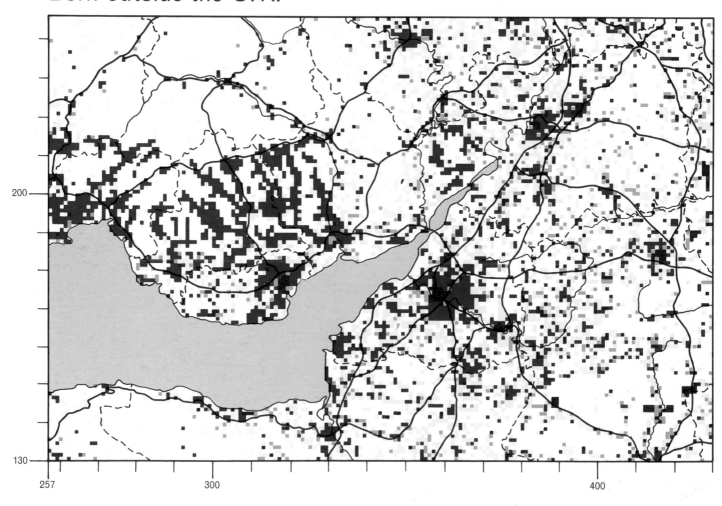

Multi-car households

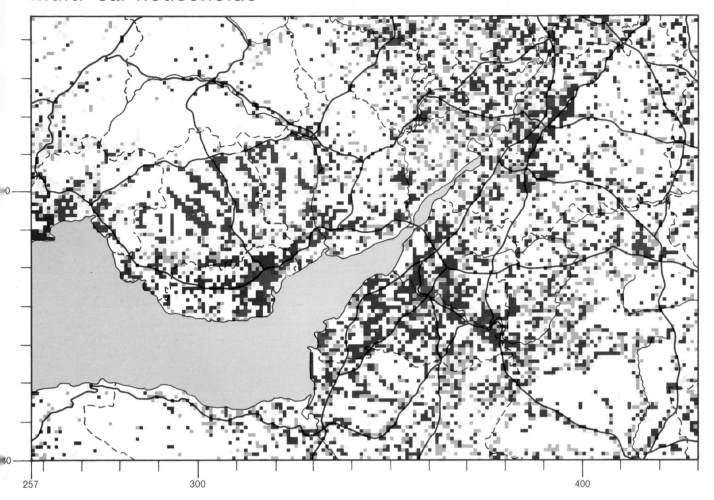

Bath deficiency

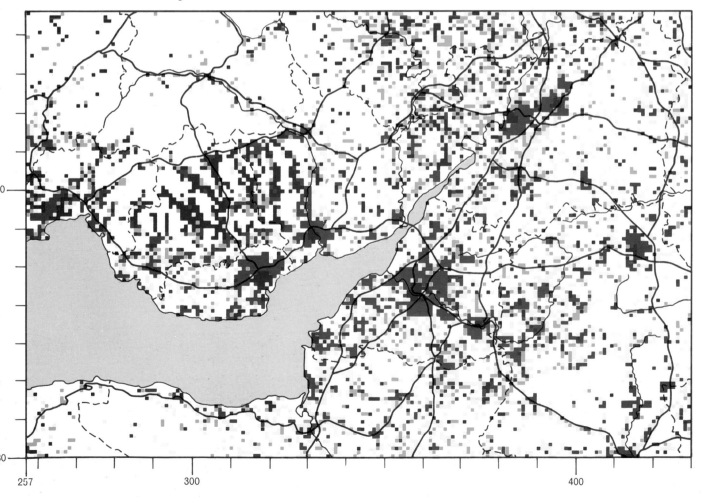

The low rural densities of much of Gwent and western Hereford and Worcester give way eastward to higher densities along the valleys and lowlands of the Wye, Severn and Avon, where market towns and service centres like Hereford, Ross-on-Wye, Tewkesbury and Evesham stand out. There is a ring of higher densities around the Forest of Dean coalfield south east of Monmouth. Cheltenham and Gloucester appear as twin cities backed to the east by the north east to south west line of the Cotswolds where low densities prevail. The main break in the Cotswold low-density area is between Stroud and Cirencester, linking with the slightly higher overall densities but very interrupted pattern of the upper valley of the Thames. Higher densities occur over much of the county of Avon, in which Bristol and its satellites are dominant. Bristol is the only urban area on the map showing the characteristic of an inner-city ring of high density surrounding a lower density core.

To the east of Avon is part of Wiltshire, with the manufacturing town of Swindon in the north, south of which stretch the large sparsely populated Marlborough Downs and Salisbury Plain, separated by the Vale of Pewsey centred on Devizes, and segmented by narrow valleys containing most of the settlements.

South of Weston-super-Mare, the settlements of the Somerset levels exhibit considerable linearity. The main town in this part of the region is Bridgwater, west of which the dominant feature is the low densities and uninhabited areas of the Quantock Hills, Brendon Hills and Exmoor, hemming in the small coastal resorts of Lynton, Lynmouth, Porlock, Minehead and Watchet.

Born outside the United Kingdom

This map is one of the five regional maps in which below average and low values predominate. Only 16 per cent of squares have high and above average values. Concentrations of high values (purple) are in the two major cities of Bristol and Cardiff, and there are lesser concentrations in Gloucester, Cheltenham, Swindon and many of the army and air force establishments on Salisbury Plain and elsewhere, particularly Tidworth, where there are children born overseas to British service families and overseas-born wives of servicemen. As for the areas with low values for people born outside the United Kingdom, the most striking are the Welsh valleys, Swansea and indeed the whole of South Wales except Cardiff. Like most other coalfields in Great Britain, the Forest of Dean has few people born abroad, as have Hereford, suburban Bristol, Weston-super-Mare and most of the part of Somerset portrayed on this map.

Multi-car households

The pattern of multi-car households indicates the distinctiveness of the various parts of the region. The red and yellow areas with low and below average levels of multi-car households stand out very clearly: the Welsh valleys; the main Welsh industrial centres – for example, central Swansea, Port Talbot, Margam, Bridgend, Barry, central Cardiff, central Newport; the most densely peopled parts of other main towns; and the military centres. In contrast, purple patches indicate high values for multi-car households in the Mumbles (south west of Swansea), the Vale of Glamorgan, Gwent, the Severn–Avon lowlands, and especially in the County of Avon around Bristol and Bath. Elsewhere, the scatter of predominantly blue and purple squares in rural areas reflects above average and high values for multi-car households.

Bath-deficient households

As in the case of many of the other regions examined in this atlas, this map of households sharing or lacking a bath is almost the reverse of the map of multi-car households. In other words, it tends to reflect many of the deprived populations rather than the more affluent ones. Consequently, the areas of high values for bath deficiency are along the Welsh valleys and in the central areas of many of the main towns, notably Cardiff and Bristol, where the cores contrast strongly with the suburban rings. On the other hand, values are more variable in the rural areas; in the Severn lowlands and to the west of the Severn above average and high values for bath deficiency are common, but in the upper Thames valley such values are rarer.

REGION 4
The English Midlands

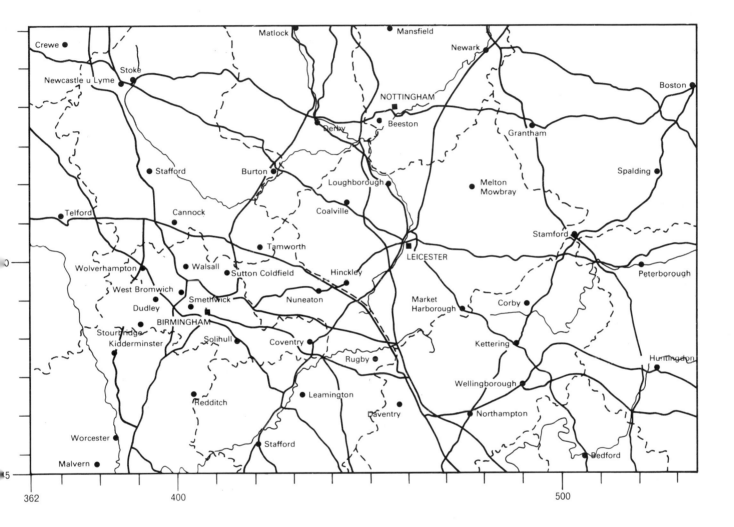

The West Midlands, focussed on Birmingham, and the East Midlands, focussed on the Nottingham–Leicester–Derby triangle, are separate Economic Planning Regions, but their core areas are close together. The maps of the English Midlands show these cores and surrounding rural areas such as the western edge of the Fens, and the scarplands and hills of Northamptonshire, Leicestershire and Lincolnshire. The maps extend from Crewe and Stoke in the north west, to Bedford and Huntingdon in the south east and Worcester and Malvern in the south west. The population of the mapped area is eight million, some 15 per cent of the Great Britain total. There are 16,665 populated squares, giving an average density of 480 per populated sq km. A fundamental distinction occurs between the rural east and the urban west and centre; the latter contains the coalfields and urban agglomerations of the Black Country, the Potteries and the southern parts of Nottinghamshire and Derbyshire and the regional centres of Birming-

ham, Coventry, Leicester and Nottingham. These centres were among the most prosperous areas in Britain during the 1960s. In the east large areas remain rural, although Peterborough, Huntingdon, St Neots and the Northamptonshire towns have undergone planned expansion.

Population density

This map is dominated by the compact concentrations of high densities in the West Midland conurbation and the other major centres. Elsewhere, higher densities mark the lines of certain trunk roads. Green squares (151–1000 people) are common in coalfield districts (for example Derbyshire and north west Leicestershire), in suburban areas and in villages. Blue squares (26–150 people) are more common in the west, especially south of Birmingham, where rural settlement is more continuously dense than in the scarplands. In the east, settlement is concentrated

[103]

Population density

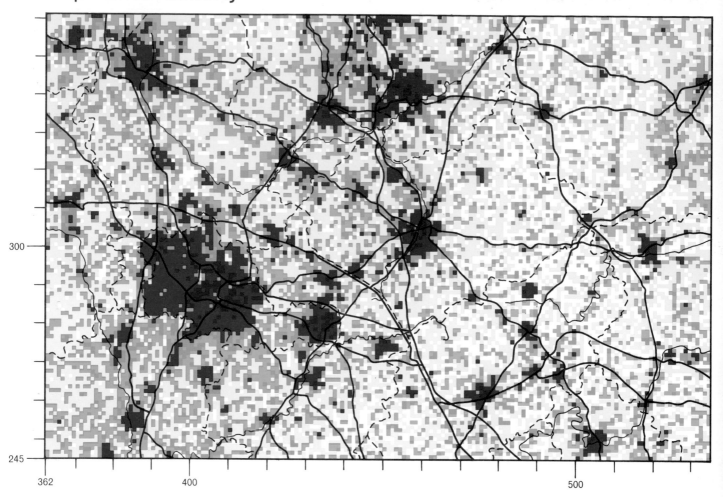

Born outside the U.K.

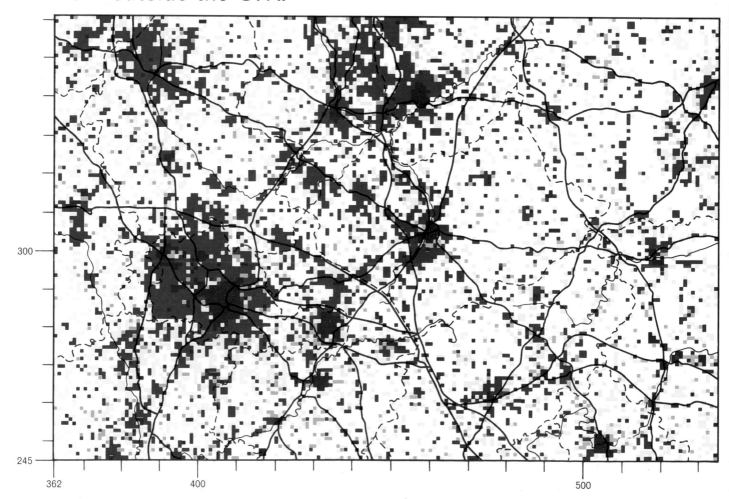

Multi-car households

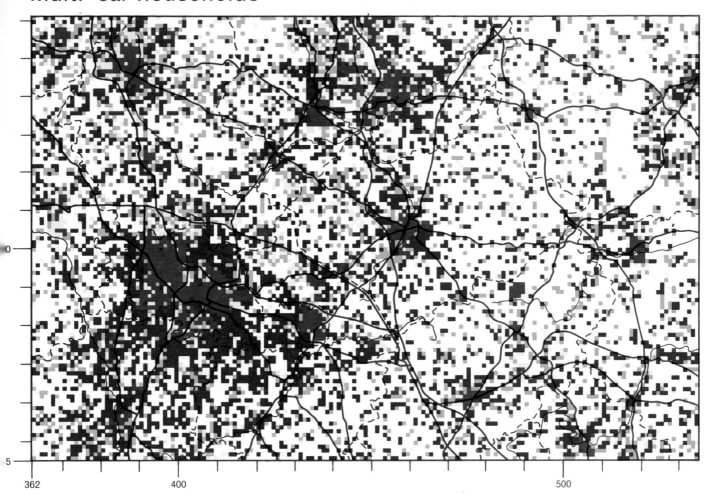

Bath deficiency

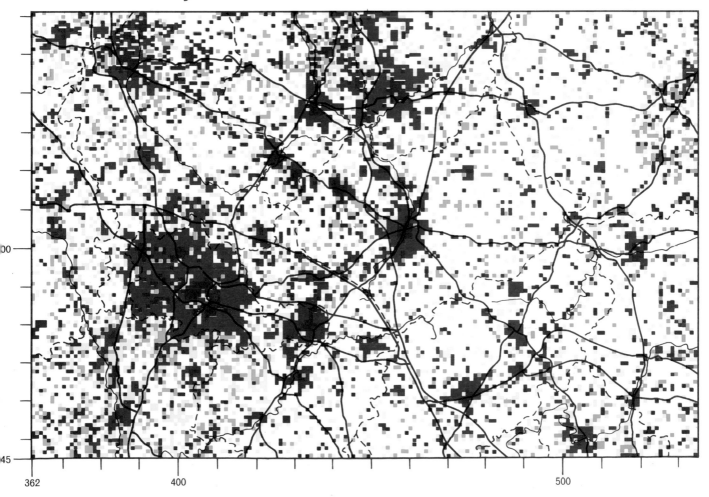

along the Nene and Ouse valleys. The line of blue and green squares running north from Peterborough and Stamford marks the Fen-edge villages along the A15 and B1177. There is little settlement in the Peat Fens, to the east of which, mapped as green and blue squares, are the straggling villages of the Silt Fens around Spalding and Boston.

Only 173 squares (black) have more than 6000 people, and 113 of these are in the West Midland Metropolitan County. These are either very closely built up or have concentrations of population in high rise developments. Their distribution is complex, though in the four largest centres of Birmingham, Coventry, Leicester and Nottingham there are loose groupings of high density areas around a core of lower density. In Birmingham, there are clusters to the north west and south east of the city centre in the Warley, Smethwick, Handsworth, Sparkbrook and Saltley districts. Further east are new estates such as Castle Bromwich. Two further groups of densely settled squares lie north of the M6, and scattered squares occur throughout southern Birmingham. West of the M5, the Dudley/Stourbridge area, with its piecemeal development, has no squares with more than 6000 inhabitants. Derby and Northampton have small concentrations, but the dispersion of the few such squares in the Potteries reflects the mixture in the six towns, of residential, industrial and open land.

Born outside the United Kingdom

While the East Midlands had a near-average proportion of people born outside the United Kingdom, the West Midlands had a higher proportion than any other Region except the South East. Concentrations of those born abroad are most marked in the inner areas of the larger cities, especially Birmingham, where a large inner area of high values contrasts not only with its suburbs (including the newer council estates) but also with the Black Country to the west. Other coalfields and older industrial areas show mainly low values, for example, in the Potteries and the districts to the north east of Derby and to the south east of Burton-upon-Trent. Other concentrations of overseas born are found in the centres of Wolverhampton, Leicester, Leamington, Nottingham and Derby and a large part of Coventry, while around Huntingdon the influence of military bases is apparent. Both Bedford and Peterborough have long established Italian communities.

Multi-car households

Multi-car households provide a clear cut pattern, being concentrated in the wealthier suburbs and under represented in central areas and council housing estates. Low values are found in Walsall, the Black Country and much of Birmingham; in the Potteries, Derby, Nottingham and the adjacent coalfield; in most of Coventry

and the whole of Corby; and in towns the size of Northampton and Burton-upon-Trent. The most extensive concentration of high values for multi-car households is around the edge of the West Midlands Metropolitan County, especially on the south side from Solihull to Stourbridge. Other blocks of high value squares are from Sutton Coldfield to the east of Walsall, on the west of Wolverhampton and to the west of Coventry. Further out, most of Warwickshire and the Severn Valley have high levels for multi-car households.

In the north, the belts of prosperous suburbs indicated by high values for multi-car households are more restricted, for example, around the Potteries. Purple squares are concentrated on the north side of Derby and to the south and east of Nottingham. Leicester has a broader suburban belt, especially to the south east. Outside the coalfields, most smaller settlements have above average or high values for multi-car households.

Bath-deficient households

This map shows the distribution of households which share or lack a fixed bath – a condition most commonly associated with poor housing and/or multiple occupation. Over the map as a whole, some two thirds of the squares are red or yellow, denoting low and below average values for bath-deficient households. High values are concentrated in a relatively small number of areas, mainly of old housing. These are most common in inner city areas, with solid blocks in Leicester, Nottingham, Derby, Stoke, Wolverhampton, Walsall and Peterborough. The corresponding zones in Coventry, Bedford, Kettering, Rugby and Stafford are less extensive, while Corby, as a New Town, is entirely lacking in such areas. Birmingham has the largest area with high values for bath-deficient households, concentrated east and north west of the city centre. Poor housing is also indicated on the coalfields, notably at Coalville and Swadlincote south of Derby. Rural areas east of Stoke, north and west of Worcester, around Spalding and east of Kettering also show patches of above average and high values for bath deficiency.

Lancashire–Yorkshire

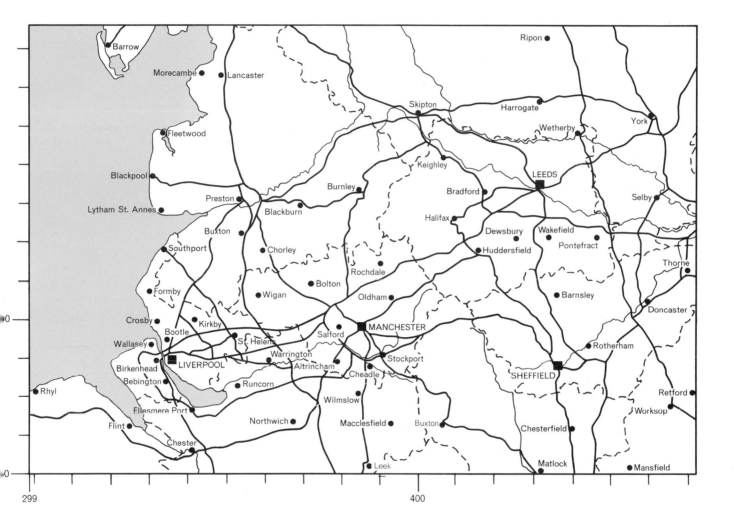

299   400

This region contains three conurbations and a major city: Greater Manchester, where the metropolitan county had a 1971 population of 2.7 million; Merseyside (Greater Liverpool) with 1.7 million; West Yorkshire, a diffuse conurbation containing Leeds and Bradford, where the metropolitan county had 2.1 million people in 1971; and Sheffield, dominating the metropolitan county of South Yorkshire, which had a population of 1.3 million in 1971. The maps also show almost all of the new county of Lancashire (1.3 million people) and much of Cheshire (0.9 million).

Population density

With 11 million people in 13,892 squares (an average density of 792 per populated sq km) the area mapped is second in density to the London region. However, the areas to the east and west of the Pennines have rarely been considered as a unit – the Pennines have formed a psychological as well as a physical barrier.

But barriers continued to be lowered in the 1970s by the construction of the motorway network with a trans-Pennine link, following earlier road, canal and rail links.

The red (and black) squares, with over 1000 people each, approximately define the urban areas which occupy such a large part of this map. The largest blocks of continuous urban development are Greater Manchester, the two flanks of the Mersey estuary, and Leeds-Bradford. The latter are scarcely separated from the southern and western towns of West Yorkshire. Both Manchester and Liverpool are separated from Warrington, but they are almost joined through Wigan, St Helens, Bolton and Bury and smaller towns between. Lines of towns follow the Don and Dearne valleys in South Yorkshire downstream from Sheffield and Barnsley, and the towns on the northern fringe of Rossendale in Lancashire almost coalesce – Accrington, Burnley, Nelson, Colne. Only

Population density

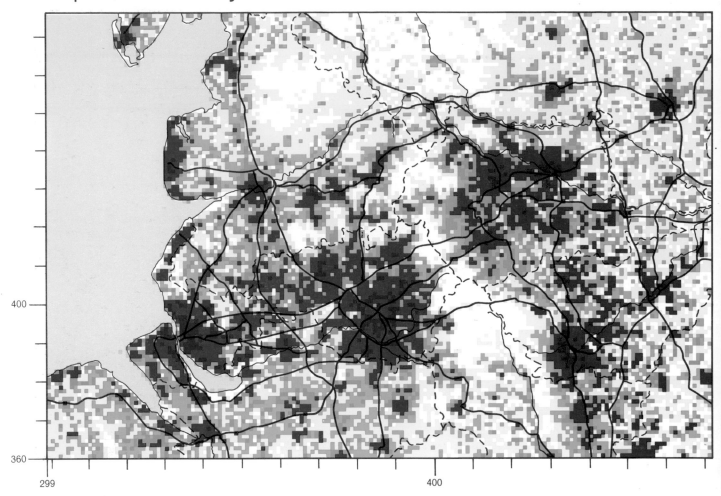

Born outside the U.K.

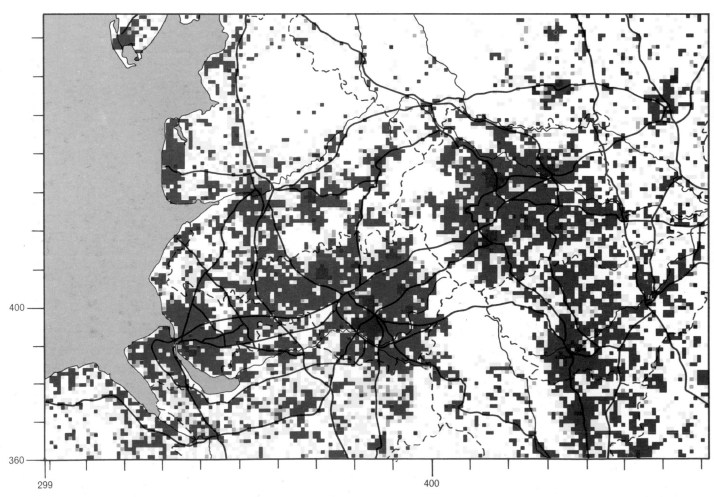

Multi-car households

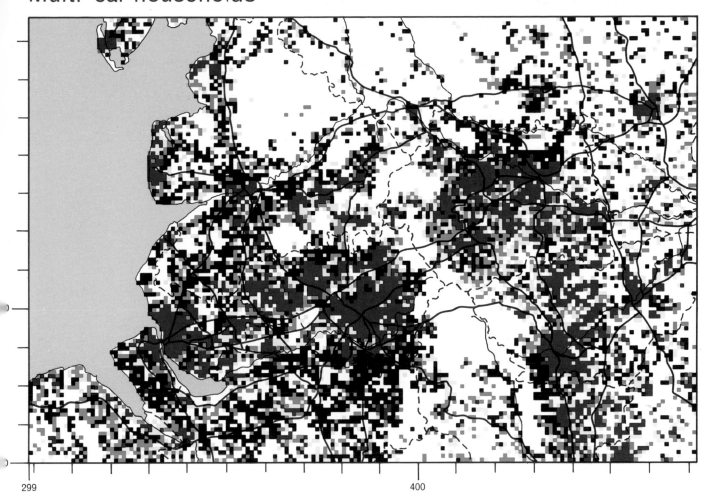

299 400

Bath deficiency

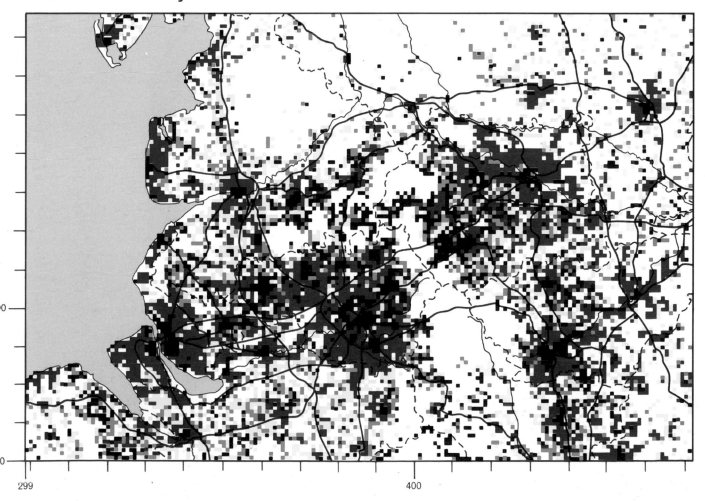

299 400

towards the edge of the map are there free standing towns such as York and Barrow.

Conurbations and towns are fringed by some green squares (151 to 1000 people), notable especially around Huddersfield, Halifax, Wigan, Chorley, Preston and Chesterfield. Blue squares (26 to 150 people each), showing dense rural settlement, are most common on the Cheshire Plain, in the former Flintshire, in west Lancashire and around Preston. Low density, often dispersed, settlement (yellow squares, with 1 to 25 people) is most characteristic of the fringe of Bowland Forest in Lancashire. It is also found in the Peak District around Buxton, north of York and west of Harrogate. Rural settlement in the Vale of York is less dense than that on the Cheshire and Lancashire Plains. There are, however, thinly populated lowland areas at Chat Moss (west of Manchester) and at Martin Mere (east of Southport), as well as along the borders of several estuaries.

In the broad urban sprawl, the black squares with over 6000 people per sq km stand out. These are either closely built up or contain such concentrations as high rise flats of various periods. The largest spread of such squares is found in Liverpool (with Bootle), forming a continuous area of 40 sq km. Manchester (with Salford) has a more intricate belt of 50 black squares around lower densities in the city centre (which is just south of the green square): the central area of lower densities, due to commerce, industry, communications and redevelopment, is well marked. Outside the central belt, small groups of black squares are found in subsidiary centres such as the Wythenshawe estate, south Stockport, Oldham, and the west side of Bolton.

While Greater Manchester has 92 squares with over 6000 people each and Merseyside has 77, West Yorkshire has only 33 and South Yorkshire 29. This is fewer than might be expected from their populations, and reflects their subdivision into separate cities and, to some extent, the broken and hilly terrain on which towns like Huddersfield are built, where areas of housing are fragmented and give lower than average densities for one kilometre squares. Only Sheffield (23 squares), Leeds (19) and Bradford (9) have large areas of high density population. By comparison, the new county of Lancashire has 34 such squares, notably in Blackpool, Preston and Blackburn.

Unpopulated squares (white) clearly outline the Pennine hills which are dissected by urban development along every valley between Bolton and Halifax. The hills are more extensive in the north (Bowland Forest and the Yorkshire Dales) and south (the High Peak, penetrated only by the valleys of Longdendale, Edale and Derwentdale). The unpopulated area is bounded approximately by the 300m contour.

Born outside the United Kingdom

This map is one of the five regional maps in which low and below average values (red and yellow) predominate. Only 10 per cent of squares have high and above average values (purple and blue). The largest continuous area of high values is in central Manchester with extensions northward and southward, but not into Salford. Bradford and Huddersfield both have areas of high values somewhat more extensive than those in the larger cities of Leeds and Sheffield. Merseyside, in particular, has very limited areas of high or above average values, as have Cheshire, the Fylde, Barrow and the coalfield areas. Small concentrations of high values for people born abroad are found in the Lancashire centres of Preston, Bolton, Rochdale, Oldham, Blackburn and some smaller towns.

Multi-car households

A strong and clear cut pattern is provided by the map showing the distribution of households with two or more cars; high and above average values are concentrated in suburban and rural areas. The distribution of multi-car households is a good indicator of prosperity and population structure although in some districts, where there is little public transport, multi-car ownership may be forced upon households with more than one wage earner. A major contrast is readily apparent between the cores of conurbations, such as Manchester/Salford and Liverpool/Bootle/Birkenhead, and their peripheries. Large central areas of cities such as Sheffield, Leeds, Bradford, Doncaster, Barnsley, Bolton, Wigan and even Blackpool and York are deficient in multi-car households.

Areas of prosperity are indicated in Cheshire, from the Wirral, through the Delamere Forest and south of Warrington to Altrincham, Wilmslow, Cheadle and east Stockport. Although the social geography of the Merseyside and Manchester conurbations is traditionally viewed as asymmetric, with less prosperity on the northern side (especially Manchester), there are definite pockets of high and above average values for multi-car households east and north west of Oldham, east and west of Swinton and in a belt north of Bury and Bolton. North of Merseyside, a zone extends from Aintree through Ormskirk to the north of Chorley and on to the north side of Blackburn. Most of the Fylde has high values but, on the coast, a contrast is visible between Blackpool and Lytham St. Annes. Likewise, Southport is distinct from the chain of settlements stretching southwards through Formby to Crosby.

In Yorkshire, there is clear asymmetry in most towns, with the indications of prosperous suburbs, for example, on the north side of Leeds and Bradford and to the west of Sheffield and Chesterfield. Much of the Harrogate and Wetherby area has high values for multi-car households.

Bath-deficient households

The distribution of households which share or lack a bath is regarded as a good indicator of poor housing. Hence this map shows the opposite end of the social scale from the map of multi-car households. Purple squares tend to be within the red areas of the previous map; they are less extensive partly because newer local authority housing is provided with amenities. In the larger cities such as Merseyside, Manchester, Leeds, Bradford and Sheffield, most of the densely populated central areas are deficient in baths, since these are areas of older or subdivided housing.

The largest cities, however, do not dominate the area of high values. Large areas of purple squares are found in St. Helens, Wigan, Bolton and the Rossendale towns, while Oldham and Huddersfield stand out prominently. An intricate pattern of bath deficiency is also found in Derbyshire and north east Wales (the former Flintshire), but close examination shows that few squares are purple on both this map and the previous one. Conversely, areas of modern suburban development, such as Wirral, south Manchester and north Leeds, have low values for bath-deficient households.

Northern England

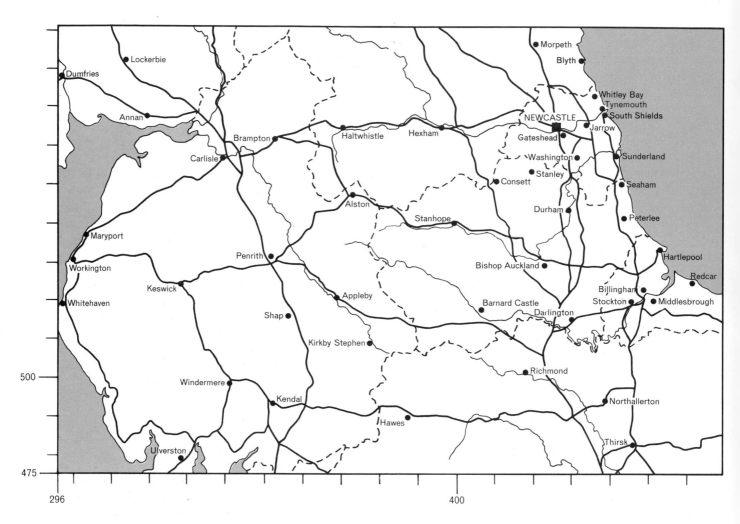

Of all the regional maps depicted in this section of the atlas, Northern England has the smallest population – 3.2 million or 5.9 per cent of the Great Britain total – of whom about three quarters live in the counties of Tyne and Wear, Durham and Cleveland – a highly distinctive area in terms of its settlement pattern and population geography. The 10,641 populated squares in Northern England have an average density of 300 per sq km, the lowest of any of the seven regions in this atlas.

Population density

Uninhabited areas (white) reflect the distribution of the main upland masses – the Pennines running from north to south across the centre of the map, the Lake District fells in the west and the North York Moors in the south east. In all these districts, population distribution is strongly influenced by relief and coloured squares mark valleys and lowlands. Thus, on the east side of the Pennines, for example, it is possible to distinguish the north-south

succession of valleys – Tyne, Derwent, Wear, Tees, Swale and Ure. Densities of less than 25 per sq km are characteristic of the main agricultural areas, covering much of the Solway Plain, the Vale of Eden, the Furness district of Cumbria and, in the east, the lower slopes of the Pennines and the plains of South Durham and north Yorkshire. Within these areas, blue squares (25–150 per sq km) mark the position of villages, but higher values are rare; the occasional red squares pick out the main market towns and service centres such as Dumfries, Annan and Lockerbie in southern Scotland, Penrith, Keswick, Windermere and Kendal in Cumbria, Hexham in the Tyne valley, Appleby in the Vale of Eden, and Richmond, Northallerton and Thirsk in North Yorkshire. The majority of squares with densities above 150 per sq km (green, red and black) are in areas of non-agricultural activity. To the west of the Pennines, the main examples are those of Carlisle, the main regional centre of the north west, and the smaller towns – Whitehaven, Workington, Maryport – of the west Cumbrian industrial zone, all of which are less striking than the extensive areas of rural territory. In the north east, however, high density squares are dominant in the coalfield/industrial zone which stretches from the top of the map to the estuary of the Tees. In this zone, densities above 1000 per sq km (red) are widespread and identify all the major urban districts – Tyneside, Sunderland, Hartlepool, Teesside and Darlington. Smaller blocks of red squares, together with a greater number of green (151–1000 per sq km) mark the dispersed and somewhat chaotic settlement pattern of the Northumberland and Durham coalfield with its numerous small towns and mining villages. Interspersed with these are numerous low density rural squares and even a few uninhabited ones.

Each of the major urban centres in the north east has its small pockets of densities over 6000 per sq km (black), among which it is possible to identify the Heaton, Walker and Scotswood districts of Newcastle, Gateshead on the south side of the Tyne, Monkwearmouth in Sunderland and Middlesbrough on Teesside.

Born outside the United Kingdom

Comparison with the maps of other regions will indicate that relatively few people born outside the United Kingdom were resident in northern England in 1971. Compared with an average of just below 6 per cent for Great Britain as a whole, the figure for the Northern Standard Region was only 1.8 per cent born abroad – some 59,000 people, of whom about 10,000 were born in the Irish Republic, 16,000 in the New Commonwealth and 33,000 in all other countries. The map is dominated by low value squares, which cover the great bulk of all urban areas and the majority of settlements in rural areas as well. Yellow and blue squares are found mainly in rural districts.

The most significant features on this map are the small numbers of high value squares. As our Great Britain maps *Born in the Irish Republic* (Map 7) and *New Commonwealth parentage* (Map 8) show, people in those groups tend to concentrate in the central districts of major urban areas, especially in the Midlands and South. In the case of northern England, the same phenomenon can be seen on a much smaller scale, in central Newcastle, in Sunderland (one square) and on Teesside. In each case, immigrants are present, together with overseas students attending centres of higher education. The latter account for the two purple squares in Durham City. Concentrations of purple squares in the south east quadrant of the map outside the main urban areas show the presence of the armed forces. The most conspicuous is Catterick military base, whose inhabitants include the foreign-born wives of servicemen and the children born to servicemen on duty overseas in Germany, Malta, Cyprus and elsewhere. It is less easy to be precise about the small numbers of purple squares in other areas. The occurrence of several such squares in the Lake District suggests the presence there of retired individuals born abroad, possibly the families of servicemen, colonial officials and diplomats.

Multi-car households

On this map, the most obvious contrast is that between the low levels of multi-car households recorded in the main urban areas and the high levels in rural districts. The most striking feature of all is the predominance of low value (red) squares in the industrial zone of the north east. High values are largely confined to peripheral areas such as Ponteland to the north west of Newcastle and recently developed districts south of Teesside, such as Ormesby and Nunthorpe. Somewhat further afield, Morpeth, Hexham and other outlying towns, which are both rural service centres and commuter towns, also have high values for multi-car households. At the same time there are several high value areas within the main built-up zone, marking places where professional and managerial workers are particularly numerous, such as Durham, Gosforth and Whitley Bay. In the north west high and above average values occur in a ring around Carlisle and throughout most of the Lake District, as in other rural areas.

Bath-deficient households

Households which share or lack a fixed bath are characteristic of older urban areas with a high proportion of low-quality housing, much of which dates from the late nineteenth century. Blocks of squares with high values for bath-deficient households are therefore prominent in the central districts of the main urban agglomerations as, for example, along both banks of the Tyne from Newcastle/Gateshead to Tynemouth and South Shields, in central Sunderland and in Middlesbrough and Stockton on Teesside. There is a scatter of high value squares on the County Durham coalfield with a marked concentration in the south west, in and around Bishop Auckland. Some of the industrial districts of West Cumbria also have high values for bath-deficient households. In contrast, there are very few such households in urban areas developed mainly since the First World War. The suburban areas of Tyneside, Sunderland, Hartlepool and Teesside are all marked by continuous blocks of red squares.

The situation in the more rural parts of the region is varied. Values close to the average predominate in most rural areas but there are some high values for bath-deficient households in some of the more remote districts, for example in upper Weardale and Teesdale. Such households are rare in rural retirement and/or commuting areas, as around Morpeth, Hexham and Keswick.

Population density

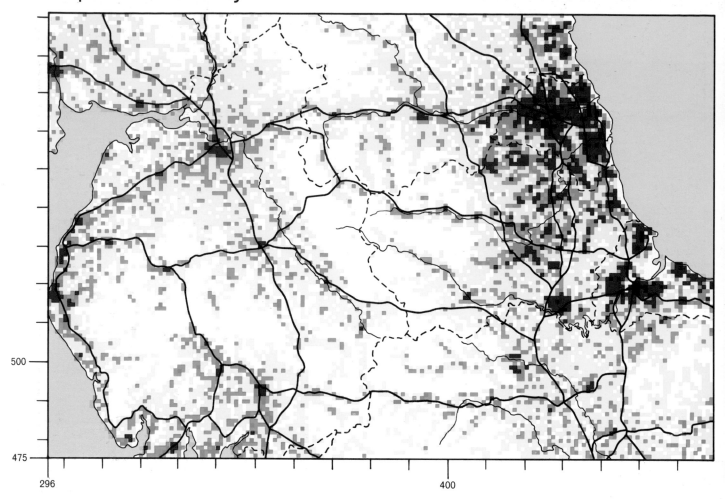

Born outside the U. K.

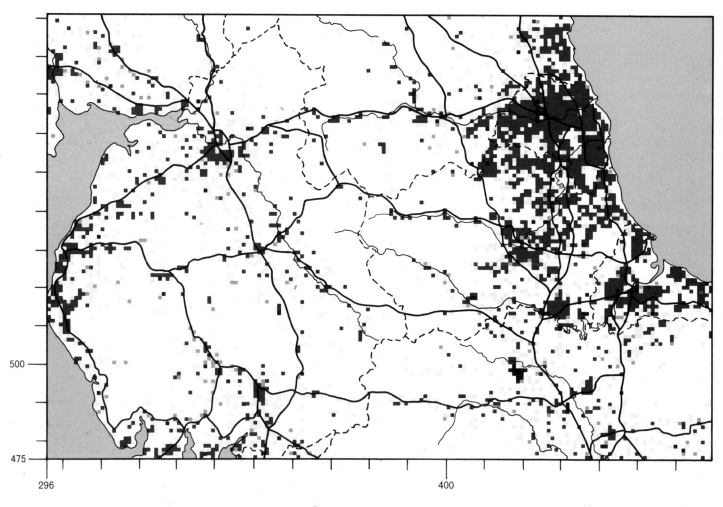

Multi-car households

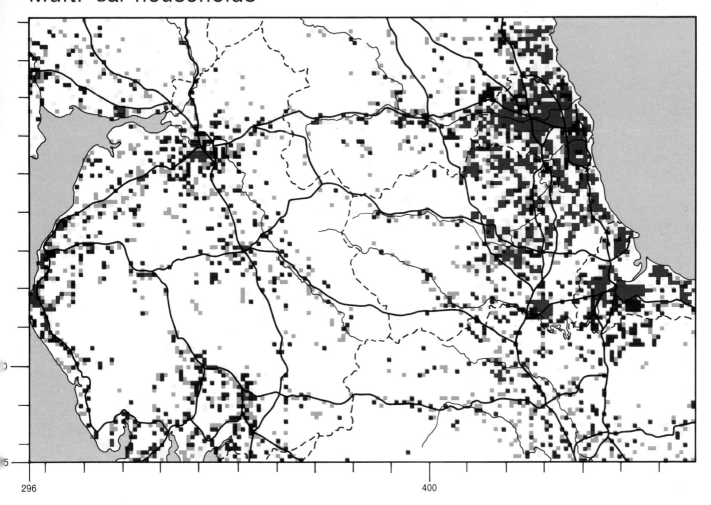

296   400

Bath deficiency

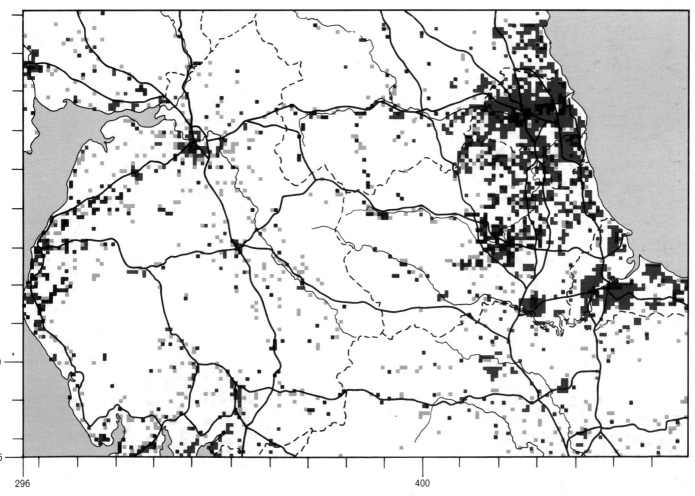

296   400

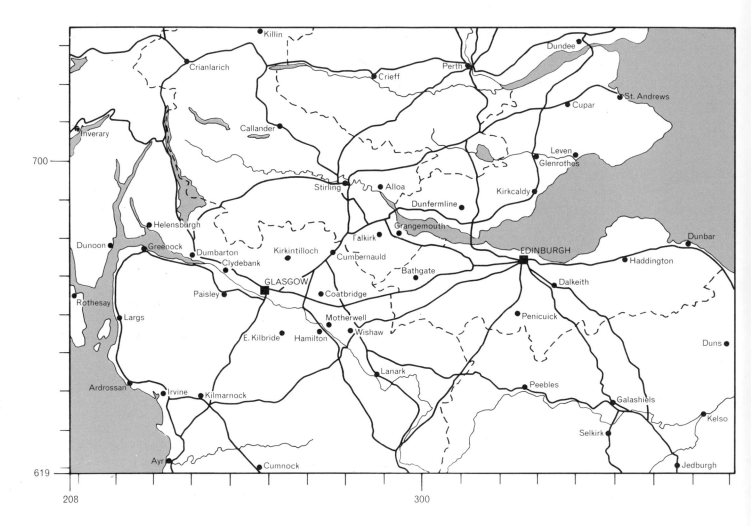

This regional map covers the bulk of the more densely populated parts of Scotland and the population of the area on the map is 4.2 million – 80 per cent of the Scottish and 7.7 per cent of the Great Britain total. Thus central Scotland is a zone of marked population concentration; the 9441 populated squares shown on the map have an average density of 445 persons per sq km. At the same time, the area displays a very wide range of population densities from extensive uninhabited areas to some of the most densely populated districts in the whole of Great Britain.

Population density

The general pattern of population distribution shows a close relationship to the relief of the area. Populated lowlands alternate with empty upland and mountain areas and there is a distinct north west to south east banding of both relief and population distribution. The north western section of the map lies within the Scottish Highlands, where narrow strings of populated squares follow the main valley routeways between the uninhabited mountain masses. To the south of this zone, a belt of settled lowland territory runs from the mouth of the Clyde to the estuary of the Tay and gives way in turn to the empty areas of the Renfrew, Kilpatrick, Campsie and Ochil hills. To the south east of this rather broken upland zone lies the main inhabited belt, extending from the Ayr lowlands to the Clyde valley and thence to the lowlands on either side of the Forth, in Fife and the Lothians. South east again, the extensive hill areas of the Southern Uplands form another zone in which population is confined to the valleys, giving way finally in the south east to the settled lowlands of the Tweed basin. In addition to these broad patterns, the use of one kilometre squares permits the identification of local features. Tents Muir, for example, a sand dune area in north east Fife, is shown as uninhabited, and a single white square near the centre of Edinburgh marks the position of Arthur's Seat.

Within the inhabited areas there are striking contrasts in population density. The extensive areas of yellow (less than 25 persons per sq km) denote the main agricultural districts, covering the lowlands of the Tay, Forth, Tweed, Clyde and Ayr basins and much of the Lothians and Fife. Within these areas, blue (26–150) and green (151–1000 persons per sq km) squares pick out the majority of rural settlement clusters and the occasional red squares (1001–6000 persons per sq km) locate such small towns as Galashiels, Jedburgh, Peebles, Cupar, Haddington and Dunbar. Larger groups of red squares denote the more important regional centres – Perth and Stirling for example – as well as the industrial districts. In addition to the major cities of Glasgow, Edinburgh and Dundee, the 1001–6000 category identifies such varied industrial areas as Buckhaven/Methil/Leven, Kirkcaldy, Glenrothes, Dunfermline, Falkirk/Grangemouth, Bathgate, Livingstone, Alloa, Dumbarton, Port Glasgow/Greenock/Gourock, Ayr/Prestwick and Kilmarnock. Squares in the highest density class (over 6000 per sq km) are very largely confined to the three biggest urban agglomerations. They are most extensive in the case of Clydeside, mainly in Bridgeton, Shettleston, Partick, Govan and Rutherglen. In Edinburgh they occur along the Firth of Forth in Leith, Newhaven and Granton and in the inner suburbs on the south side of the city, where nineteenth century tenement buildings predominate. In Dundee, only a few scattered squares reach this level.

Born outside the United Kingdom

Of the entire population of Scotland in 1971, only 2.6 per cent, some 135,000 people, had been born outside the United Kingdom: about 30,000 each in the Irish republic and New Commonwealth, and 75,000 in all other countries. The great majority of these people live in the area covered by the map of Central Scotland. The limited number of people born overseas seem to be concentrated into a few areas. Low value (red) squares predominate, covering practically all the main urban-industrial areas as well as the majority of smaller settlements.

There are, however, a number of exceptions. Blocks of high value squares occur in central districts of both Edinburgh and Glasgow, where, for example, Scotland's very small groups of immigrants from New Commonwealth countries are concentrated and where there are also students from overseas. High values are also associated with military establishments, as around Holy Loch on the Clyde. A few high value squares also occur in rural areas, probably in some cases marking the retirement homes of people of Scottish origin born overseas, in others marking establishments with overseas born workers or guests.

Multi-car households

The possession by a household of more than one car may gener-

ally be considered as a sign of prosperity, though multi-car ownership may also result from deficiencies in the public transport system. For the latter reason, the great majority of rural areas show high (purple) or above average (blue) values and there are remarkably few in the low category. At the other end of the scale, low proportions of multi-car households are characteristic of urban industrial areas, where many sizeable towns are almost entirely within this class, for example, Buckhaven/Methil/Leven, Kirkcaldy, Dumfermline, the towns of the Fife coalfield, Falkirk/Grangemouth, Dumbarton, Port Glasgow/Greenock/Gourock and Kilmarnock. New Towns also display low values. In contrast, smaller settlements within commuting range of the cities show high values, for example those near the southern end of Loch Lomond and on the northern side of the lower Clyde estuary. In the case of the major cities there are strong internal variations. The Clydeside conurbation as a whole is characterised by low levels of multi-car ownership, but there are zones with high values, one on the north side of the conurbation around Bearsden, the other on the south along the A77 Glasgow–Kilmarnock road. In Edinburgh, high values predominate in the west and south, in Corstorphine, Colinton and Liberton.

Bath-deficient households

The map of households which share or lack a fixed bath is in some ways a mirror image of the map of multi-car households; though areas where local authority housing is prominent can have low values for multi-car households and very low values for bath-deficiency. Rural areas for the most part show values not significantly different from the national GB average and the major contrasts are between and within the various urban areas. Most striking are the high values recorded in the densely populated inner areas of the major cities: Glasgow, Edinburgh and Dundee all have central blocks of purple squares surrounded by extensive areas of low values. Elsewhere, squares with high values for bath-deficient households occur only in very small clusters, for example along the Fife coast from Kirkcaldy to Leven and in Perth, Stirling, Paisley, Hamilton, Motherwell, Wishaw and Kilmarnock.

As the maps of the whole of Great Britain in the earlier part of this atlas show, many of the variables mapped have significantly different values in Scotland from those recorded in England and/or Wales. Nevertheless the patterns displayed on these maps of the most densely populated part of Scotland show similar contrasts to those found elsewhere in Britain; contrasts between rural and urban areas, between industrial towns and service centres, between city cores and suburban fringes and between declining settlements and New Towns.

Population density

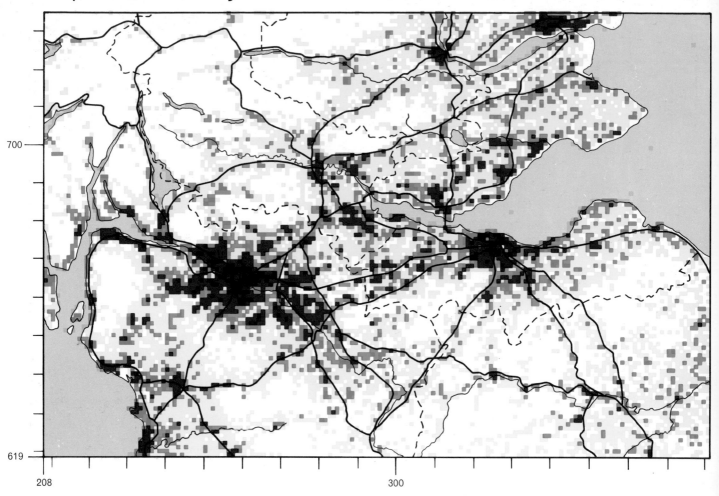

Born outside the U.K.

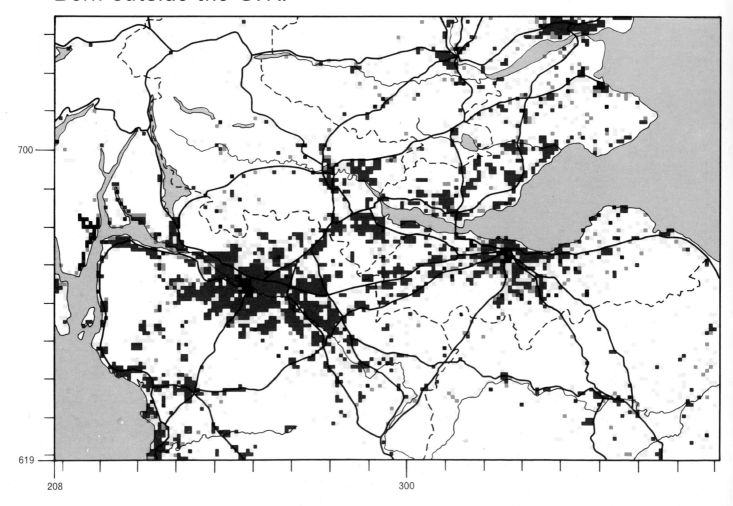

Multi-car households

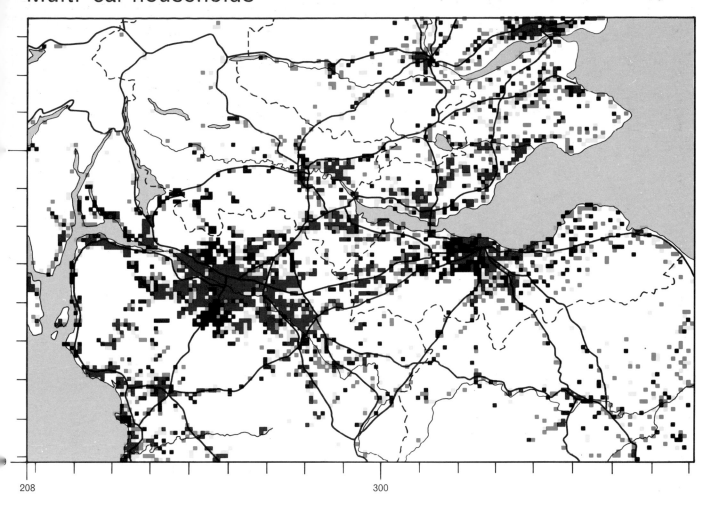

Bath deficiency

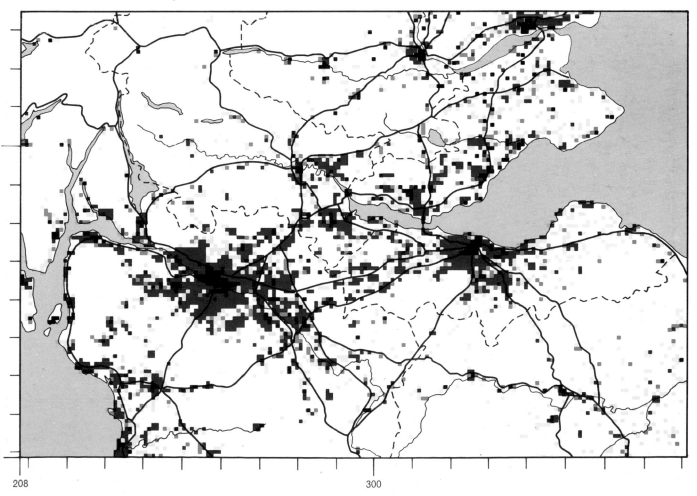

Appendices

1 Definitions of the variables selected for mapping

2 The use of the signed chi-squared measures for mapping

3 National and regional averages for the variables mapped

4 The distribution of squares among mapping classes

5 Publications of the Census Research Unit

Definitions of the variables selected for mapping

Following is a list of the variables mapped in this atlas and their definitions in terms of the original census data. In the case of the absolute number maps indicated by an asterisk in the list below (see Introduction page 6), the variables as defined are mapped in classes based on their numerical values. In the signed chi-squared maps (the great majority of the GB maps and three of each set of four regional maps) the values of the variables as defined are allocated to classes by the method described in Appendix 4.

Map title	Map number	Definition
Population density*	3	Persons, per sq km.
Born in Scotland*	5	Persons born in Scotland, per sq km.
Born in Wales*	6	Persons born in Wales, per sq km.
Born in the Irish Republic*	7	Persons born in the Irish Republic, per sq km.
New Commonwealth parentage*	8	Person with both parents born in the New Commonwealth *plus* persons born in the New Commonwealth with at least one parent born in the New Commonwealth, per sq km.
		The New Commonwealth was all the countries of the Commonwealth in 1971 except Australia, Canada and New Zealand, which have become known as the Old Commonwealth. In 1971, Pakistan (comprising West and East Pakistan) was a member of the Commonwealth, and is therefore included in 1971 Census figures.
Sex composition	9	Males, per 10,000 total population.
Fertility of young married women	10	Number of children ever born to married women aged 16–29 years in private households, per 1000 such women.
Children	11	Persons aged 0–14 years, per 10,000 total population.
Persons over retirement age	12	Males aged 65 and over *plus* females aged 60 and over in private households, per 10,000 people.
Type of age structure	13	See text accompanying map.
Educational qualifications	14	People in employment with
		i) GCE A level qualifications or equivalents and/or
		ii) higher qualifications (broadly Higher National, nursing, teaching, degree and senior professional or vocational qualifications), per 10,000 employed people. Some people with certain qualifications (for example, GCE A levels and a degree) were included in both groups.
Foremen and skilled manual workers	15	Foremen and skilled manual workers (socio-economic groups 8 – foremen and supervisors, manual; and 9 – skilled manual workers), per 10,000 economically active in civilian employment.
Unskilled manual workers	16	Unskilled manual workers (socio-economic group 11), per 10,000 economically active in civilian employment.

Farmers, foresters and fishermen*	17	Persons employed in agriculture, forestry and fisheries, per sq km.
Miners*	18	Persons employed in mining and quarrying, per sq km.
Manufacturing workers	19	Persons employed in manufacturing industry, per 10,000 employed.
Managerial and professional workers	20	Managerial and professional workers (socio-economic groups: 1 – employers and managers in central and local government, industry, commerce, large establishments; 2 – employers and managers, small establishments; 3 – self-employed professional workers; 4 – professional workers, employees; and 13 – farmers, employers and managers), per 10,000 economically active in civilian employment.
Unemployed men	21	Unemployed males, per 10,000 economically active males.
Car to work	22	Persons travelling to work by car, per 10,000 employed.
Bus to work	23	Persons travelling to work by bus, per 10,000 employed.
Train to work	24	Persons travelling to work by train, per 10,000 employed.
Walking to work	25	Persons travelling to work on foot, per 10,000 employed.
Owner-occupiers	26	Owner-occupied households, per 10,000 private households.
Council tenants	27	Council-rented households, per 10,000 private households.
Private tenants	28	Unfurnished and furnished privately rented households, per 10,000 private households.
Household amenities	29	Households with exclusive use of a hot water system, fixed bath and inside WC, per 10,000 private households.
Households with no car	30	Households with no car, per 10,000 private households.
Overcrowding	31	Households with more than one person per room, per 10,000 private households.
Spacious dwellings	32	Households with less than 0.5 persons per room, per 10,000 private households.
One-person households	33	Households consisting of only one person, per 10,000 private households.
One-parent families*	34	Families consisting of one parent and one or more dependent children, per sq km.
Born outside the UK	Regions	All residents present at Census, born outside the UK, per 10,000 present resident population.
Multi-car households	Regions	Households with more than one car, per 10,000 private households.
Bath-deficient households	Regions	Households which share or lack a fixed bath, per 10,000 private households.

*These variables are mapped on an absolute numbers basis; the rest are mapped by the signed chi-squared method.

The use of the signed chi-squared measure in mapping

The introduction to this Atlas (pages 6, 7) discusses the problem of mapping a variable which is closely correlated with the total population – for example, numbers of old people. A map showing absolute numbers of old people would present a spatial pattern not appearing to differ much from a map showing absolute numbers of the total population. Plotting the ratio of the numbers of old people to the total population leads to different problems when the absolute numbers of people in kilometre squares vary over very wide limits. This is because, particularly in sparsely populated areas, the ratio is subject to erratic variations. Although we do not suggest that the inhabitants in a particular grid square have been drawn at random from a large population, such a notion of randomness does in fact provide a useful basis for analyses of these fluctuations, treating them as sampling errors. Variations in the ratio are greater in squares with smaller populations, and they may partially or wholly mask important patterns – rather as noise may swamp a radio signal.

Suppose that the national proportion of the population with a given characteristic (for example, aged 60 or over) is π and that the population in each one of a set of grid squares is n. Then, if the given population characteristic were randomly distributed amongst the population of all the grid squares, the observed proportion with the given characteristic in a grid square – call this proportion p – would be distributed binomially around the mean π with a standard deviation σ, where

$$\sigma^2 = \pi(1-\pi)/n \quad \ldots \ldots (1)$$

The more sparsely populated the area (that is the smaller the value of n), the larger would be the value of σ, and the more widely would the observed proportions p vary about the mean value π.

While the distribution of characteristics amongst the population may, in practice, differ markedly from random, so that the binomial distribution postulated will not apply, it is still the case that the observed values of p will vary more widely in areas with small populations. This limits the usefulness for mapping of the ratio or proportion.

The introduction has described the disadvantages of presenting the statistics in a different way: a map showing, for each grid square, the difference between X, the observed number of people with a given characteristic, and the number that would be expected if the proportion with that characteristic in the grid square were the same as the proportion in the country as a whole. Writing the expected proportion as π, such a map would plot $(X-\pi n)$ or $(p-\pi)n$, where n is the population of the grid

square and p is the observed proportion with the given characteristic. This can be written as (O–E), the observed number less the expected number. However, the absolute difference between observed and expected numbers of people with a characteristic can never be large for a square with few people. This limits the usefulness of this second kind of map.

Thus neither plotting the proportion of people with a given characteristic nor plotting the difference between observed and expected numbers with that characteristic is wholly satisfactory. The compromise we have adopted for some 25 of the variables in this atlas is to calculate the value for sub-groups of population or households.

$$X^2 = \frac{(O-E)^2}{E} \quad \ldots \ldots (2)$$

Summation over sub-groups gives the X^2 statistic. It has the additional advantage over the other methods that it can be used when several population sub-groups are of interest, for example, for the study of age composition.

It is necessary also to know whether deviation from the national average is positive or negative. By retaining the sign of (O–E), we define the quantity 'signed chi-square', X_s^2.

In the binomial case, where there are only two sub-groups in a population, those with a certain characteristic and those without, the value of X^2 can be written as follows.

$$X^2 = \frac{(np-n\pi)^2}{n\pi} + \frac{(n(1-p)-n(1-\pi))^2}{n(1-\pi)}$$

$$= \frac{(p-\pi)^2 n}{\pi(1-\pi)} \quad \ldots \ldots (3)$$

Hence, from (1)

$$X^2 = \left[\frac{p-\pi}{\sigma} \right]^2 \quad \ldots \ldots (4)$$

The maps

The signed chi-squared maps show four colours. Where we are interested in only one characteristic, *purple* signifies that X^2 exceeds 3.84 and that the observed proportion is higher than the national proportion, so that X_s^2 exceeds 3.84. The legend on the map in this case is 'high'. *Blue* signifies that X^2 is less than 3.84 and that the observed proportion is higher than the national proportion, that X_s^2 is between 0 and 3.84. The legend is 'above average'. Thus both purple and blue denote the squares in which the observed proportion is higher than the national proportion.

Yellow and red denote the squares in which the observed proportion is lower than the national proportion. *Yellow* signifies that X^2 is less than 3.84, and X_s^2 is between 0 and -3.84. The legend is 'below average'. *Red* signifies that X^2 exceeds 3.84, that is X_s^2 is less than -3.84. The legend is 'low'. The significance of the value 3.84 is discussed below.

As explained in the introduction and illustrated in the diagram on page 7, while the dividing line between blue and yellow represents a constant ratio or proportion (the national average proportion), the dividing lines between purple and blue, and between yellow and red, do not represent constant proportions but rather constant values of chi-squared, $X^2=3.84$. The diagram on page 7 shows that a grid square with a chosen proportion lying above the national average would be coloured purple if the square were sufficiently densely populated, but would be coloured blue if the square were sparsely populated. The words *high* and *low* in the legend of the chi-squared maps refer not to the magnitude of the proportion of the deviation of the observed proportion from national proportion but to the magnitude of chi-squared.

If a single population characteristic being studied were randomly distributed among the population, values of X^2 in excess of 3.84 would occur, by chance, in 5 per cent of the grid squares. It is on this basis that the cut-off value of $X^2=3.84$ has been chosen to separate purple from blue and yellow from red. A statistician finding in a particular grid square a value of X^2 exceeding 3.84 might say that the observed proportion in the grid square was significantly different from the national proportion 'at the 5 per cent level'. Dropping the qualification implied by these last six words, it might be said, with rather less precision, that the squares coloured purple were those in which the proportion was *significantly* greater than the national proportion; and that the squares coloured red were those in which the proportion was *significantly* less than the national proportion.

Such an interpretation, however, depends on the assumption that the characteristic being studied is randomly distributed among persons or households. Such an assumption may often be untenable. For example Map 9 shows the proportion of males. Males are not distributed in anything like a random way because of the frequency of occurrence of married couples; these tend to reduce the variability of the male proportion. On the other hand, the presence in some areas of institutions of predominantly one sex such as military establishments tends to increase the variability of the male proportion. In fact, Appendix 4 (Table 2) shows that 5.29 per cent of the grid squares fall in the purple and red categories taken together, compared with the 5 per cent of squares which would

fall in these categories if males were distributed randomly throughout the whole population. That the number of purple and red squares should be so near to the theoretical 5 per cent of all squares is fortuitous, reflecting on the one hand the restricted variability of the male proportion due to the frequency of occurrence of married couples, and on the other hand the real differences in the male proportion between different regions and areas as described in the text accompanying Map 9.

To give another example, households renting their accommodation from local authorities are in no sense randomly distributed among households. This is because local authority housing tends to occur in sizeable blocks rather than in single units. Hence, even if local authority housing represented an essentially constant proportion of housing throughout the country, its 'lumpy' presence in relation to one kilometre grid squares would mean that many more than the theoretical 5 per cent of squares would be coloured purple or red – the actual proportion of such squares are 17.85 per cent and 59.82 per cent respectively.

The conclusion to be drawn is that, though the chi-squared criterion adopted in the maps (whether X^2 is less than or greater than 3.84) relates to a well-established test of statistical significance, the assumptions underlying the test are likely to be satisfied by few if any of the variables mapped. Accordingly, any inference that squares coloured purple or red represent areas in which the observed proportion differs in a statistically significant way from the national proportion needs to be heavily qualified.

The technique adopted accepts that a given absolute deviation is more noteworthy in a smaller population, while a given proportionate deviation is more noteworthy in a larger population. The colour classes on the maps must be interpreted in relation to the signed chi-square scale, and not in terms of absolute deviations or proportionate deviations.

National and regional averages for the variables mapped

National average values for the variables mapped in the atlas are given in the Great Britain column of the table below. Where the texts accompanying the maps refer to 'above average' or 'below average' values, the reference is to these national averages.

Regional averages are also given in the table, but it must be emphasised that these are for the eight *Standard Regions* of England, together with Wales and Scotland and not for the regional areas mapped individually in the atlas.

Definitions of all the variables are given in Appendix 1.

Mapped variable	Map no.	Great Britain	North	Yorkshire and Humberside	North–West	East Midlands	West Midlands	East Anglia	South–East	South–West	Wales	Scotland
Population density	3†	235	45	302	877	211	363	114	589	153	126	66
Born in Scotland	5†	1025	206	137	134	185	129	139	179	135	68	9166
Born in Wales	6†	538	37	53	116	85	216	81	157	292	8220	21
Born in Irish Republic*	7†	130	30	70	140	90	180	60	210	80	50	60
New Commonwealth parentage*	8†	230	40	180	120	210	410	80	430	80	40	30
Sex composition	9	4853	4882	4871	4829	4931	4947	4926	4821	4823	4861	4809
Fertility of young married women+	10	1200	1230	1250	1280	1200	1220	1180	1110	1210	1270	1320
Children	11	2396	2469	2442	2475	2450	2502	2324	2270	2290	2369	2591
Persons over retirement age*	12	1600	1540	1590	1600	1520	1380	1730	1630	1860	1670	1490
Educational qualifications	14	1999	1652	1554	1777	1619	1657	1738	2309	1963	1859	2641
Foremen and skilled manual workers	15	2462	2883	2886	2531	3141	2862	2288	1995	2209	2663	2595
Unskilled manual workers	16	783	983	897	893	690	750	708	646	688	927	993
Farmers, foresters and fishermen	17†	269	319	250	120	311	223	862	154	555	447	409
Miners	18†	166	472	412	65	508	125	22	18	83	476	171
Manufacturing workers	19	3453	3408	3870	4121	4082	4773	2812	2905	2719	3113	3218
Managerial and professional workers	20	1358	1106	1150	1219	1182	1211	1402	1631	1489	1196	1183
Unemployed men	21	419	619	448	491	356	365	378	323	349	457	649
Car to work	22	3564	3122	3179	3406	3774	3919	4241	3542	4320	4137	2913
Bus to work	23	2470	3237	3339	3134	2460	2656	1098	1857	1532	2379	3462
Train to work	24	634	182	87	290	55	108	87	1565	74	126	341
Walking to work	25	2088	2341	2103	2115	2192	2113	1943	1850	2362	2161	2458
Owner-occupiers*	26	4830	4070	4840	5350	5090	5030	5090	4920	5580	5390	2940
Council tenants*	27	3030	3860	3210	2790	2890	3340	2700	2430	2340	2310	5340
Private tenants*	28	2120	2060	1950	1860	2020	1620	2210	2610	2070	1680	1720
Household amenities*	29	8250	8170	8230	8000	8040	8360	8220	8270	8580	7750	8630
Households with no car*	30	4900	5750	5620	5450	4730	4600	3950	4550	3970	4680	5770
Overcrowding*	31	720	780	590	630	510	670	390	620	450	500	1920
Spacious accommodation*	32	3270	3010	3370	3490	3700	3340	3880	3240	3850	3860	1870
One-person households*	33	1820	1780	1880	1880	1650	1570	1720	1930	1770	1670	1860
One-parent families	34†	883	874	859	982	823	785	778	909	847	827	906
Born outside the UK	Regional	587	183	380	409	459	638	500	1006	413	239	256
Multi-car households	Regional	870	579	632	698	867	970	1124	1037	1104	860	587
Bath-deficient households*	Regional	1220	1060	1150	1130	1110	990	1240	1320	1010	1480	1320

*These variables appear in the original Census statistics as whole numbers per 1000 and have been multiplied by 10 to give values per 10,000. Thus the figures given here are to the nearest 10 per 10,000.

+In the case of fertility of young married women, the original statistics were given per 100 and are expressed here per 1000.

†For the absolute number maps the variables are shown per 10,000.

APPENDIX 4
Distribution of squares among mapping classes

As explained in the introduction, the preparation of the maps in this atlas involved the allocation of each one-kilometre square to a pre-determined class; these classes differ as between the various types of map. The three tables in this appendix indicate the class intervals used and the numbers and/or proportions of squares falling into each class for all our Great Britain and regional maps with the exceptions of Map 1 *Populated squares* and Map 2 *Unsuppressed squares,* which are single-class maps, Map 9 *Sex composition* and Map 13 *Types of age structure,* which use special systems of classes explained in the accompanying texts.

Absolute number maps
Table 1 shows, for each absolute number map (a) the class intervals by the minimum and maximum count included in each class; (b) the total number of populated squares (Maps 3 and 4) or unsuppressed squares (the remaining maps) for which data of the variables are available, together with the number falling into each of the four or five mapping classes; and (c) the number of squares in each class as a percentage of the total squares mapped. It should be noted that only integer values of the variables are possible in all absolute number maps. The last three absolute number maps (Map 17 *Farmers, foresters and fishermen;* Map 18 *Miners;* and Map 34 *One-parent families*) are based on 10 per cent sample data, and the sample values have been multiplied by 10 and thus only integers describable in tens can occur; hence the broad gaps *between* classes. Except for Map 17 *Farmers, foresters and fishermen,* the class intervals have been defined to approximate to geometric progressions, with limits rounded to simple figures. For Map 17, an arithmetic progression has been used, with an open-ended upper class which includes fewer squares than the other classes.

In each absolute number map, the number of squares per class decreases rapidly from lower to higher classes. Thus, despite the geometric progressions of class intervals, the strong positive skewness of these variables is still portrayed geographically by the concentration of squares into lower classes. This is particularly marked for miners (Map 18) and people of New Commonwealth parentage (Map 8) because of the regional and local concentration. People born in Scotland (Map 5) and those born in Wales (Map 6) are more widely spread, partly because such people are present in larger numbers.

It should be noted that the meaning of a count of zero differs between variables for which a full 100 per cent count is available with suppression (population and birthplace) and variables for which only 10 per cent sample data are available (Maps 17, 18 and 34). For the 100 per cent variables (Maps 5 to 8) zero means that, despite a total population of 25 or more in the square, there are no individuals of the specified type; nevertheless in suppressed squares (those with a total population of 24 or less) there might, in theory, be up to 24 people of the specified type. The yellow squares therefore denote absence of members of the group being mapped while blank squares indicate the suppression of data. For 10 per cent variables (Maps 17, 18 and 34), however, zero simply means that none of the specified type was present in the sample, but such persons might be present unsampled. It is therefore less important, in the last three variables, to distinguish yellow squares from suppressed squares.

Table 1 gives, in addition to the national totals (which include the numbers in suppressed squares), the maximum numbers in a single square. These show, for example, that the New Commonwealth population reaches higher densities than the Irish or even the Welsh.

Signed chi-squared maps
Table 2 gives corresponding results for chi-squared maps, all of which have the same system of class limits related to the *national* average and the (arbitrary) critical chi-square value of 3.84. The skewness of some frequency distributions is nevertheless apparent, for example, in the large proportion of squares falling in the lowest class of Map 30 *Households with no car,* and in the highest class of Map 29 *Household amenities.* The distribution of council tenants (Map 27) and owner-occupiers (Map 26) is such that most squares fall in the two extreme classes, especially the lowest class for the former (with its urban bias) and the highest class for the latter. For most 10 per cent variables, especially foremen and skilled manual workers (Map 15) and unskilled manual workers (Map 16), few squares fall outside the near average classes. Here, positive skewness is revealed by concentration in the class just below average, for example, (Map 23) *Bus to work,* (Map 24) *Train to work,* (Map 25) *Walking to work,* (Map 19) *Manufacturing workers* and (Map 14) *Educational qualificiations.* The 100 per cent variables – unemployed men (Map 21) and overcrowding (Map 31) – show a similar pattern.

Because of the greater incidence of suppression a smaller number of squares is mapped for the 10 per cent sample variables than for the 100 per cent variables. Among the latter, the number of squares mapped for household variables is slightly greater than that for population variables. Fewer squares are available for Map 10 *Fertility of young married women,* because some unsuppressed squares have no married women aged 16–29 years.

Regional maps

Table 3, for the regional maps, completes the picture. For the population maps the number of squares in each of the five classes is given, but for the others (signed chi-squared maps, with four classes) the number of squares per class is given only as a percentage of total number of unsuppressed squares; this provides a better basis for comparison between regions.

In the maps of London and the English Midlands most of the squares (84 per cent) are populated. These areas have little or no sea. But the maps of Central Scotland and Northern England have large areas of moorland in addition to sea, and only about half the squares have any population. In each of the other three areas mapped about 70 per cent of the kilometre squares are populated.

Roughly half the populated squares on the regional chi-squared maps are suppressed. This is less than the national incidence of suppression and reflects the denser populations of the areas chosen for regional enlargement. Northern England is most affected by suppression, followed by Central Scotland. Much less affected are Lancashire–Yorkshire, the Central South Coast and especially London.

The map of the Central South Coast has a large overlap with the London map (most of Greater London is repeated) and hence characteristics of the mapped areas are very similar. London and the Central South Coast have the largest number of very densely populated (over 6000 per sq km) squares, followed by Lancashire–Yorkshire which in fact has slightly more squares with 1001–6000 people.

Regional differences are particularly marked in the case of people born outside the United Kingdom. Such individuals are particularly concentrated in the London and Central South Coast regions, which have more than one fifth of their grid squares in the highest class. Regional contrasts are also strong in the case of multi-car households, with an even distribution of squares between classes in Northern England and Central Scotland but 59 per cent in the top class in London and the Central South Coast. Relatively few grid squares have concentrations of bath-deficient households, and these are most numerous in England outside the south east.

TABLE 1 Absolute number maps of Great Britain

Map	Variable		(a) National total, and (b) Maximum per square		(a) Number of classes and (b) Number of mapped squares		(a) Class intervals, (b) Number of squares in each class, and (c) Percentage of mapped squares in each class				
3	Population	a	53,978,540	a	5	a	1–25	26–150	151–800	801–4000	over 4000
	(density)	b	24,286	b	*147,685	b	82,044	34,866	15,737	11,326	3712
						c	55.55	23.61	10.66	7.67	2.51
4	Population	a	53,978,540	a	5	a	1–2,500	2,501–15,000	15,001–80,000	80,001–400,000	over 400,000
	per 10 km sq	b	897,265	b	*2697	b	1206	862	466	130	13
						c	44.72	31.96	17.28	5.56	0.48
5	Born in	a	5,386,866	a	4	a	0	1–10	11–50	over 50	
	Scotland	b	16,790	b	67,546	b	24,663	21,948	12,822	8113	
						c	36.51	32.49	18.98	12.01	
6	Born in	a	2,825,934	a	4	a	0	1–10	11–50	over 50	
	Wales	b	8559	b	67,546	b	26,948	22,999	11,131	6468	
						c	39.90	34.05	16.48	9.58	
7	Born in the	a	693,441	a	4	a	0	1–10	11–50	over 50	
	Irish	b	2321	b	67,546	b	38,149	19,825	6738	2834	
	Republic					c	56.48	29.35	9.98	4.20	
8	New	a	1,209,222	a	4	a	0	1–10	11–50	over 50	
	Commonwealth	b	9645	b	67,546	b	47,540	13,383	4146	2477	
	parentage					c	70.38	19.81	6.14	3.67	
17	Farmers,	a	634,970	a	5	a	0	10	20	30	over 30
	foresters and	b	300	b	54,153	b	30,615	13,064	6021	2533	1920
	fishermen					c	56.53	24.12	11.12	4.68	3.55
18	Miners	a	391,480	a	5	a	0	10	20–40	50–110	over 110
		b	1160	b	54,153	b	46,108	3622	2273	1241	869
						c	85.14	6.76	4.20	2.29	1.60
34	One parent	a	627,410	a	5	a	0	10	20–30	40–70	over 70
	families	b	760	b	54,153	b	36,276	7489	5022	3421	1945
						c	66.99	13.83	9.27	6.32	3.59

*Squares with one or more people

TABLE 2 Signed chi-squared maps of Great Britain

Map	Variable	National average percentage	Number of mapped squares		(a) Number of squares, and (b) Percentage of mapped squares in each class			
					Value of signed chi-square			
					−3.85 and below	−3.84 to 0	0 to 3.84	+3.85 and above
9	Sex composition	48.53	147,685	a	4055	139,875		3755
				b	2.75	94.71		2.54
10	Fertility of young married women	1.20 (children)	58,479	a	5060	25,745	20,703	6971
				b	8.65	44.02	35.40	11.92
11	Children	23.96	67,546	a	14,524	23,117	17,824	12,081
				b	21.50	34.22	26.39	17.89
12	Persons over retirement age	16.00	65,021	a	13,240	16,099	17,602	18,080
				b	20.36	24.75	27.07	27.81
14	Educational qualifications	19.99	53,277	a	6145	24,759	11,706	10,667
				b	11.53	46.47	21.97	20.02
15	Foremen and skilled manual workers	24.62	53,308	a	3583	28,106	16,764	4855
				b	6.72	52.72	31.45	9.11
16	Unskilled manual workers	7.83	53,308	a	2349	36,015	10,761	4183
				b	4.41	67.56	20.19	7.85
19	Manufacturing workers	34.53	53,277	a	6400	29,883	11,277	5717
				b	12.01	56.09	21.17	10.73
20	Managerial and professional workers	13.58	53,308	a	4258	23,473	16,109	9468
				b	7.99	44.03	30.22	17.76
21	Unemployed men	4.19	67,533	a	7584	41,879	11,366	6704
				b	11.23	62.01	16.83	9.93
22	Car to work	35.64	53,277	a	4346	17,021	21,225	10,685
				b	8.16	31.95	39.84	20.06
23	Bus to work	24.70	53,277	a	8085	32,405	8053	4734
				b	15.16	60.82	15.12	8.89
24	Train to work	6.34	53,277	a	6391	39,560	3830	3496
				b	12.00	74.25	7.19	6.56
25	Walking to work	20.88	53,277	a	5855	27,754	13,054	6614
				b	10.99	52.09	24.50	12.41
26	Owner occupiers	48.30	68,422	a	17,007	10,905	13,378	27,132
				b	24.86	15.94	19.55	39.65
27	Council tenants	30.40	68,422	a	40,927	10,609	4675	12,211
				b	59.82	15.51	6.83	17.85
28	Private tenants	21.20	68,422	a	18,855	15,258	14,021	20,288
				b	27.56	22.30	20.49	29.65
29	Household amenities	82.50	68,422	a	13,954	13,235	16,379	24,854
				b	20.39	19.34	23.94	36.32
30	Households with no car	49.00	68,422	a	35,338	19,032	6518	7534
				b	51.65	27.82	9.53	11.01
31	Overcrowding	7.20	68,422	a	13,517	36,056	11,674	7,175
				b	19.76	52.70	17.06	10.49
32	Spacious accommodation	32.70	68,422	a	9112	15,040	24,728	19,542
				b	13.32	21.98	36.14	28.56
33	One person households	18.20	68,422	a	12,784	31,143	17,478	7017
				b	18.68	45.52	25.54	10.26

TABLE 3 Regional maps

	Central South Coast	London	South Wales– Severnside	English Midlands	Lancashire– Yorkshire	Northern England	Central Scotland
Population							
Total number of populated squares	13,985	16,632	13,435	16,665	13,892	10,641	9,441
Percentage of map area	70.70	84.08	68.07	84.25	70.23	53.80	47.73
Class limits and number of squares in each class							
0 — 25	4475	5777	6877	7893	5287	6953	5918
26 — 150	4181	4492	3614	4211	3252	1942	1544
151 — 1000	2643	3231	1867	2496	2395	917	927
1001 — 6000	2166	2588	1016	1892	2681	749	903
over — 6000	520	544	61	173	277	80	149
Born outside the United Kingdom							
Suppressed squares	4478	5778	6993	7988	5310	7227	6128
Unsuppressed squares	9681	11,051	6763	8967	8751	3808	3630
Class limits of signed chi-square and percentage of squares in each class							
−3.85 and below	20.64	24.82	38.84	44.43	58.82	51.81	49.83
−3.84 to 0	36.02	37.25	45.26	40.23	31.61	41.60	37.71
0 to + 3.84	20.31	16.57	10.63	8.10	4.86	4.54	8.10
+3.85 and above	23.03	21.36	5.26	7.25	4.72	2.05	4.35
Multi-car households							
Suppressed squares	4378	5668	6911	7886	5313	7214	6155
Unsuppressed squares	9781	11,161	6845	9069	8748	3821	3603
Class limits of signed chi-square and percentage of squares in each class							
−3.85 and below	9.33	8.58	10.07	12.65	26.45	22.77	29.20
−3.84 to 0	10.05	10.32	18.26	14.83	18.36	22.40	23.20
0 to +3.84	21.74	22.28	28.77	25.48	21.39	27.69	25.23
+3.85 and above	58.87	58.81	42.91	47.04	33.80	27.14	22.37
Bath-deficient households							
Suppressed squares	4378	5668	6911	7886	5313	7214	6155
Unsuppressed squares	9781	11,161	6845	9069	8748	3821	3603
Class limits of signed chi-square and percentage of squares in each class							
−3.85 and below	38.37	38.09	24.66	32.46	39.47	30.36	41.13
−3.84 to 0	37.01	33.13	36.52	32.04	26.86	36.01	36.50
0 to +3.84	12.70	14.48	20.85	18.26	14.09	16.91	11.05
+3.85 and above	11.92	14.30	17.97	17.23	19.57	16.72	11.32

APPENDIX 5

Publications of the Census Research Unit, Department of Geography, University of Durham

A Working papers

1 J I Clarke, *Population and Scale,* 1975, £1.

2 I S Evans, J W Catterall and D W Rhind, *Specific transformations are necessary,* 1975, £1.

3 D W Rhind, *Geographical analysis and mapping of the 1971 UK Census data,* 1975, £1.

4 M Visvalingam, *Storage of the 1971 UK Census data: some technical considerations,* 1975, £1.

5 J I Clarke and D W Rhind, *The relationship between the size of areal units and the characteristics of population structure,* 1975, £1.

6 M Visvalingam, M J Norman and R Sheehan, *Data interchange on industry-compatible tapes,* 1976, £1.

7 M Visvalingam and B J Perry, *Storage of the grid-square based 1971 GB Census data; checking procedures,* 1976, £1.

8 M Visvalingam, *Chi-square as an alternative to ratios for statistical mapping and analysis,* 1976, £1.

9 D W Rhind, I S Evans and J C Dewdney, *The derivation of new variables from population census data,* 1977, £2.

10 M Visvalingam and J C Dewdney, *The effects of the size of areal units on ratio and chi-squared mapping,* 1977, £2.

11 D W Rhind, K Stannes and I S Evans, *Population distribution in and around selected British cities,* 1977, £1.25.

12 M Visvalingam, *A locational index for the 1971 kilometre-square population census data for Great Britain,* 1977, £1.25.

13 J Coulter, *Grid square census data as a source for the study of deprivation in British conurbations,* 1978, £2.

14 M Visvalingam, *The identification of demographic types: a preliminary report on methodology,* 1977, £2.

15 J Mohan, *The use of grid-square census data in the location of hospital facilities: a case study of the Durham Health District,* 1980, £2.

B Special Publications

J C Dewdney and D W Rhind, (Editors), *People in Durham — A Census Atlas,* £3.

Copies of both working papers and special publications may be ordered from:

Administrative Assistant and Map Curator
Department of Geography
University of Durham
South Road
DURHAM DH1 3LE
England

Printed in England for Her Majesty's Stationery Office
by Linneys of Mansfield Ltd. Dd 597295 K36 3/80.